Success
REIMAGINED

INSPIRING STORIES OF LOCAL LEADERS

Internet addresses given in this book were accurate
at the time it went to press.

Printed in the United States of America

Published in Hellertown, PA

Cover and interior design and illustrations by Christina Gaugler

Library of Congress Control Number 2021901221

ISBN: 978-1-952481-08-6

2 4 6 8 10 9 7 5 3 1 paperback

BrightCommunications.net

To the Lehigh Valley Local Luminaries

featured here, whose stories

of success reimagined are so inspiring

Contents

Introduction

Success comes in surprising packages, some small, some big, some looking odd at first glance. And success is not a place that is arrived at in a linear chart, nor does it reveal itself quickly. This book is a parade of stories. And how this idea was hatched and borne is fascinating as well.

The greatest part of my job is the amazing people I meet. The day I met Rita Guthrie was one of the most fortunate days of my career. Rita, the Idea Lady, helped me to reimagine my own success, in ways I never thought possible. All my life I have struggled with shyness, sitting in meetings with my stomach in knots at the thought of having to introduce myself, worrying for weeks or months before I had to give a presentation. After spending time with Rita and attending her Marketing Academy, I surprised myself with my newfound courage. After applying my knowledge, I no longer dreaded public speaking. I wanted to talk! In fact, I had to restrain myself. Suddenly, I found my voice, my vision was clear. Who was this new me? As I spoke, my world expanded, and my newfound confidence attracted more and tremendous opportunities. As I reinvented myself, I no longer saw myself as a "small" publisher.

Another fortunate day was when Rita introduced me to Rob Sayre. Rob and I instantly connected through our shared experiences at Rodale, Inc., and our passion for serving others and developing our vision of success. Like Rita, Rob quickly became a mentor and a friend. I learned that success is not always linear, one step after another. Often success comes in leaps and

Success is to be measured not so much

by the position that one has reached in life

as by the obstacles he has overcome.

—Booker T. Washington

bounds. I knew a leap was coming when Rob shared an idea; "There are so many amazing, talented people here in the Lehigh Valley! Why don't we bring their stories and advice together in a book?" It was a flash of insight and inspiration. We invited Rita to join us to launch this book. We are so proud of the stories of business leaders in our area.

Over the next few months, our vision became a clear, actionable plan. Rob and Rita reached out to business leaders in the Lehigh Valley, inviting them to be part of our Local Luminaries program. These leaders shared their stories with our terrific and talented writer Marie Susznyski. They shared personal successes, business successes, business successes that led to personal successes, and personal successes that led to business success. They shared their stories, tips, advice, and fascinating journeys of success and how they reimagined their own lives.

We added Terree O'Neill Yeagle to our team, capturing images of our local business leaders. Pictures are indeed worth a thousand words and these photos show just what success looks like.

We are proud to present these Lehigh Valley Local Luminaries stories here. We've not ordered them alphabetically, nor by degree of success or business category, but rather in the way we think can be best savored. May this book inspired you to achieve your own success!

—Jennifer Bright

With Kenyan Roots and a Strong Work Ethic, I Brought a Well-Known Franchise to the Lehigh Valley

Jimmy Olang, franchise co-owner with wife, Jessica, of The Brothers That Just Do Gutters-Lehigh Valley

Growing up in Kenya, I was taught that success was going to college and becoming a doctor, lawyer, or engineer. But I lived in a small village called Oyugis, where we farmed the land, raised goats and sheep, collected water from the river, and walked miles to go to school. I didn't see success—in the traditional sense—in my future.

And it's true that I didn't become a doctor, lawyer, or engineer, but I worked hard to achieve a level of success I never imagined. I'm co-owner with my wife of a multimillion-dollar company, The Brothers That Just Do Gutters-Lehigh Valley.

I lived with my grandmother in Oyugis until I was 12, while my father worked toward a business degree in the United States. When he came back to Kenya, I moved to Nairobi to live with him, my mother, and my siblings.

But eventually the economy experienced a downturn, and my dad's consulting business collapsed, like many others. He decided to go back to the United States while I stayed behind. During that time, my local church hosted U.S. missionaries. Ken Parsons, the founder of The Brothers That Just Do Gutters, was one of them. I became friends with Ken, and when he left, he told me he wanted me to work for him if I ever moved to America.

In 2001, I did just that. I moved to the Hudson Valley region in New York. Very quickly, Ken sought me out at church and offered me a job on the

I worked hard to achieve a level of success I never imagined.

spot. He had founded his business hanging gutters in 1999. His brother, Ryan, joined him in 2002.

I had a lot to learn. When Ken told me I'd be hanging gutters, I asked, "What are gutters?" I grew up in a hut with a thatched roof. I showed up for the first day of work wearing flip-flops and was told I needed to buy boots for the next day. I had never been involved in home remodeling, but I was used to climbing trees, so getting onto a roof wasn't an issue.

I earned minimum wage as Ken's apprentice, and I poured my heart and my soul into the work. Like many immigrants who come to the United States, I worked two or three jobs. I also earned an associate's degree while working.

I met my wife, Jessica, in 2009. I was looking to settle down and hoping I'd find love in church or a library, like it happens in movies. Love came to me, though, through a Christian dating site. We got married, and Jessica moved from the Lehigh Valley to the Hudson Valley.

As time went on, Jessica and I realized working so much wasn't going to be sustainable. At the same time, Ken was growing his business and was starting franchises. After 13 years of working for him, Jessica and I decided we wanted to branch out on our own. We moved to the Lehigh Valley and officially launched our Brothers Gutters franchise. We're one of 15 franchises under the company.

Since then, we've grown from one truck, one apprentice, and a 10-by-10 foot office space to now having seven trucks and 20 employees. We've created a successful, balanced life between working hard and having time for our family of four children.

My Success Reimagined

I never thought I'd be a business owner. My dream was to work hard and earn American dollars. But the day I set foot in this country, I had incredible opportunity that, combined with hard work, helped me get to where I am today.

Being a husband-wife team was also key to our success: Many small businesses have trouble growing because they're stuck in the day-to-day work of running the company. As general manager and sales manager, Jessica had the ability to get a bird's-eye view of the company. Getting that bigger picture allowed us to make long-term plans for growth.

■ **We make an impact on our community:** Launching our business has transformed our lives, and we make an effort to do the same for the people who work for us. Our employees have opportunities to be

Launching our business has transformed our lives, and we make an effort to do the same for the people who work for us.

promoted and achieve success. One of our employees has been with us since our first month and is doing very well.

We also work with and donate to charities and organizations, such as the Allentown Rescue Mission. We do everything we can to have an impact on our communities, employees, and their families.

What I read: Books are part of the Brothers' culture. Our installers have a skills ladder that allows them to grow to become team leaders. Along the way, they read books to master the soft skills of customer service and life lessons. One of the books they read is *Raving Fans* by Ken Blanchard and Sheldon Bowles.

One of the books I've read and enjoyed on my own is *Cashflow Quadrant: Rich Dad's Guide to Financial Freedom* by Robert T. Kiyosaki. One of Jessica's reads is *QBQ! The Question Behind the Question: Practicing Personal Accountability at Work and in Life* by John G. Miller.

I also listen to *Grow with the Bros*, a podcast started by The Brothers That Just Do Gutters franchise.

ASR Media: Telling the Stories of the Lehigh Valley

Ashley Russo, four-time Emmy award–winning executive producer and owner of ASR Media Productions, host of *The PEAK TV* and *St. Luke's HealthNow*, and creator and host of *Unscripted with Russo*, a podcast featuring the personal stories behind VIPs

Telling stories has always been very important to me. While attending New York University, I worked at the college radio station and interned for public relations and media companies. During school and immediately following, I spent some time in front of the camera but was really drawn to the behind-the-scenes production work. The singular role of finding and telling stories, writing, interviewing, and problem solving is what drew me to media production.

My earliest mentors were my mother and grandmother. They introduced me to the meaningful rewards that come from giving back. When I first moved to the Lehigh Valley, a parent with two young children, I became an active community volunteer and fundraiser to meet new people and find personal fulfillment. It didn't take long to discover the unique strength and reach of our local nonprofits. The combination of my media skills and connections through this work prompted the launch of ASR Media Productions.

In 2012, an opportunity to produce local television content presented itself. Then Vice President of Marketing for St. Luke's University Health Network, Ken Szydlow, asked me to create a half hour pilot that would feature feel-good stories of health, wellness, and community. I found four simple stories, paid day rates to a few video production teams and an editor, and cobbled together an episode to present to WFMZ – Channel 69. The station's general manager, Barry Fisher, was pleased and *The PEAK TV*, sponsored by St. Luke's, began airing on Sunday evenings in September of that year.

That project quickly escalated into a full-fledged production company, ASR Media Productions, with a mission to share positive, impactful, and uplifting stories. Because the Lehigh Valley is such a vibrant, growing area, remarkable stories of hope and inspiration aren't hard to find. ASR Media tells stories of patients walking again as a result of spinal cord rehab, educators assisting students who have experienced trauma, veterans finding healing and love with help from therapy dogs, and so much more.

In addition to feel-good health and wellness stories, there were opportunities to create video content for local businesses and organizations, with storytelling at the center. ASR Media also sponsors video production for local nonprofits, and the team and I actively participate in their work.

There have been a few bumps along the way. The work of turning out 28 minutes of content every week for *The PEAK TV* was arduous and required tight deadlines. One of the biggest challenges early on was managing the work. I shed many tears and lost a lot of sleep questioning if I could build a successful television and video production company with talented people who shared my vision. With the help of brilliant colleagues at St. Luke's and my fledgling team, we churned out weekly shows on a wing and a prayer. Over the next year, I established a clear and intentional vision, defined goals, and nurtured and grew a team that would align with my business model.

The Key to My Success

Bringing structure to the process was key to my business success. I've established processes and procedures to meet production deadlines, and I'm continuously improving upon them. If something goes wrong, we review the procedure, identify the issue, update the steps, and communicate the change to staff.

ASR Media went on to form partnerships with other local powerhouse organizations like the Greater Lehigh Valley Chamber of Commerce, *Lehigh Valley Style* magazine, United Way of the Greater Lehigh Valley, and more. My initial hire, Katie Wallace Santana, is now ASR Media's Vice President of Production and Operations, managing the daily needs of clients and a staff of nine.

I learned that being true to myself and producing good work, of which I'm exceptionally proud, will always lead to my reimagined success.

■ **Destined for this business:** My mother said I was a talkative kid who asked a lot of questions—a natural fit for journalism. I grew up in central New Jersey, the oldest in a large, blended family. Balancing time between two families, four parents, and nine siblings taught me management skills early on and fostered my interest in people. I also yearned to be part of a team, often in a leadership role. I joined any activity I could, from field hockey to musicals to the school paper.

Bringing structure to the process

was key to my business success.

How I schedule my time: Part of my success comes from maximizing my day. My business coach, Shawn Hayashi, reminds me that we have only 168 hours in a week, and it's up to us how we use them. I start by scheduling family activities and exercise to guarantee I make time for myself and loved ones. Then I prioritize my team, scheduling standing team meetings and one-on-ones. I book time for running the business and time for simply thinking—something I don't take for granted. Finally, I squeeze in filming, client calls, and some space for inevitable last-minute, yet crucial items that come up every week.

What I do in my free time: I'm a third-generation champion equestrian and have passed down my love of horses to my daughter, Renna. My family, which also includes my husband, Joe, and son, Nolan, and I enjoy outdoor activities, including golf and tennis, as well as traveling and spending time together watching movies on our pop-up movie screen.

What I read and listen to: Time in the car, getting ready for the day, folding laundry, or making dinner all present opportunities to fill my mind with positive and inspiring audiobooks. I love listening to books by the brilliant and courageous Brené Brown and leadership expert Jim Collins. I could listen to Simon Sinek, who writes about inspiration, or Gino Wickman, an entrepreneur who helps businesses thrive, every day.

One of my favorite books is *Atomic Habits* by James Clear, and my current read is *Maybe You Should Talk to Someone* by Lori Gottlieb.

Nonprofit work today: I proudly serve on the boards of United Way of the Greater Lehigh Valley, Wildlands Conservancy, Greater Lehigh Valley Chamber of Commerce, Children's Home of Easton, and Hospital Central Services, Inc. & Affiliates.

Leadership awards: I am a Girl Scouts of Eastern PA's Take the Lead honoree and was recognized with United Way of the Greater Lehigh Valley's Community Builder award. I also received the Golden Laurel award from the YWCA of Bethlehem and the Betsy Torrence Philanthropist of the Year award from Women United. Actively nominating and supporting my peers and up-and-coming young women is important to me, and it brings me immense satisfaction when they receive accolades for their work.

I Traded My Suit and Tie for a Caribbean Dream

Mike Sosnowski, co-owner with wife, Marisol, of PRX Club,
a Puerto Rico experience club and wedding venue

I've always had an open mind and a deep curiosity, and that led me down the path to launching a dream business: hosting groups at our rental properties in Puerto Rico—complete with stunning views of the Caribbean—and taking our guests on one-of-a-kind tours of the island.

I've been a serial entrepreneur for most of my life, running a cleaning company, a food assembly kitchen, and a staffing company for nuclear medicine, all in the Lehigh Valley.

I met my wife while studying for a degree in nuclear medicine. We talked about what we ultimately saw ourselves doing in life. She said she'd love to have a bed-and-breakfast, and I said I'd love to live in a Spanish-speaking place. Her parents are from Puerto Rico, so opening a B&B in Puerto Rico was a natural choice.

We made the jump when we bought a house tucked into the mountains of Patillas, two minutes from the beach and with panoramic views of the Caribbean Sea. We rented the studio apartment on the bottom level of our home to host travelers looking for a unique Puerto Rico experience, including seeing sights an average tourist wouldn't normally see, such as a trip into the mountains to see how roosters are raised for fighting and to restaurants where they'll eat authentic cuisine.

I don't give a laundry list of activities to our clients. Instead, I hand-tailor an experience for that particular group. When people are interested in booking with us, I send a survey to find out what they're interested in and create an itinerary just for them.

An Amazing Opportunity

From the beginning, our plan was to find additional properties for PRX. We stumbled on an amazing opportunity to buy another place in the municipal-

ity of Patillas, which is on the southeastern coast of the island. We're remodeling the property to get it ready for more rentals, and we invited a few people to see it. One of them asked if they could host a wedding there. All of a sudden, our remodeling plans went up a notch. We're creating a space that can also host weddings of 60 to 70 people.

Anyone who wants to have a unique Caribbean experience is our ideal client. We've hosted travelers from Canada, Spain, and the United States, from Boston to California. We've even had interest from people who want to move to Puerto Rico permanently, and we're open to using our rental properties as places for people to use during their transition to living on the island.

My wife, Marisol, is a perfect co-owner and partner. We have very different skill sets that balance each other out.

I knew for a long time I was geared toward starting a business. After graduating from college, I took a job as an accountant, but I realized quickly I wasn't a suit and tie guy, and I didn't like sitting behind a desk all day. So, I got a backpack and went to South America with the plan to travel until I ran out of money. During my first week in Chile, I was asked to teach English, and I ended up living there for a year.

But I really credit two key things to my success: having curiosity and humility. I have a drive to learn about everything, and I'm always asking questions. I think my pool contractor is afraid I'll start my own pool company because I hang out with his guys and ask about their work. When I was younger, I'd offer to help friends build a deck or put in a paver patio so I could gain the experience and knowledge. I'm also not afraid to confess I don't know something or to ask for help. I've realized that people will go out of their way to share what they know.

▨ **My advice for other entrepreneurs:** Remember that business ideas should be in pencil, not pen. The world is always changing, and our ideas should change, as well. I once read a perfect example of why quitting can be necessary sometimes: If you're moving toward a cliff, there's nothing wrong with turning around and retracing your steps. The key is to keep moving, even if you backtrack for a bit.

I really credit two key things to my success:

having curiosity and humility.

The world is always changing,
and our ideas should change, as well.

Also, there are no shortcuts. The truth is, very few people will do what it takes to start their own business and be successful. It takes a tremendous amount of effort, forward thinking, and ability to cut through the noise in media and on social networking sites.

Thirty years ago, the bookstore had a self-help section that was one row with 50 books. I'd read them all while drinking coffee. Today, the self-help section has grown to several aisles, and the number of books available is endless. It's harder to get at the truth of something because there's too much information. The message has become more complex, and it's harder to get the 30,000-foot view that helps crystalize an idea.

I have a large group of friends in their twenties who aren't sure how to navigate the business world. They try something and then jump off and try something else. It takes patience. You have to have an open mind and be curious, take it all in, and draw your own conclusions.

My mentors: There are too many to name. Everyone has something to offer if you ask the right questions. I learn and grow by modeling other people, and when I meet someone who approaches business or life in a negative way, I know what not to do.

How I set my daily schedule: I've been fortunate to have an innate ability to organize and prioritize my days. I see what needs to be done and when I want to accomplish it. Then I reverse engineer to figure out a schedule to get it done.

What I've read and watched recently: *The Accidental Billionaires: The Founding of Facebook* by Ben Mezrich. Many people don't know Mark Zuckerberg's backstory. He was laser-focused and never made excuses. Also, TED Talks and YouTube videos that explain how things work are my entertainment outlet.

For 20 Years, My Goal Remains the Same: To Empower Women through Fashion and Connection

Jill Strickland Brown, owner and visionary of Frox in Perkasie, storyteller, and author of *Behind the Button*

The large, deep, beautiful windows are what originally drew me to the space where I opened Frox in 2003. I had been a sales rep for many clothing manufacturers in seven mid-Atlantic states, but then 9/11 happened. I wanted to be close to family and open my own shop in my hometown in case something happened again. I wanted to offer luxurious women's clothing and home décor.

From the beginning, my goal at Frox has been to empower women and make them feel good about themselves, and that starts before they even walk into the shop. Our themed window displays, which change every month, are designed to inspire women. One month, we may celebrate "every-body" by displaying photos of our clients holding glittering apples or pears representing their own body shape. Another month, we'll create an elaborate display of water bottles cut into flowers, telling the story of recycling and making the ordinary extraordinary. Our windows are a looking glass to the world.

Once customers are in the shop, they'll find unique, on-trend clothing and home items that I've personally chosen. I scour New York City markets and showrooms and meet with local and international artisans to find the perfect items that we carry in Frox.

As our customers shop, we do everything we can to make it an amazing experience, from the sunny goldenrod yellow walls to the modern industrial but warm décor. The fitting rooms—where the magic happens—make our clients feel pampered within the luxurious surroundings.

Women remember us because they come in as strangers and leave as friends, looking and feeling great. Our style team has specialized knowledge of the lines we sell. We always find the perfect fit and create a flattering silhouette for our gals.

We're located in Perkasie, a borough with a population of fewer than 9,000. But we have a customer list of more than 7,600 people who have visited our shop over the years. Part of that success came because the experience of shopping at Frox is so memorable. Our shoppers rave about us.

When my family first moved here, there were only a few businesses. One of the first things I did was join the Perkasie Town Improvement Association, an organization that supports local businesses. I worked with other shop owners and the economic director to help attract an interesting array of shops and emporiums. The town has blossomed into the "hidden gem of Bucks County."

Perkasie has the oldest Christmas tree lighting ceremony in the country, our seasonal farmers' market, and our August car show. These events bring thousands of people into town.

I organize my own events at the store to take advantage of the foot traffic. Every year at Christmas, a violinist sets up and plays in our window, creating a wonderfully festive atmosphere that draws people into the store.

But celebrating our customers is something we do year-round. We host parties, fashion shows with customer-models, and other events, complete with cocktails and food. I'm always looking for ways to invite people into the shop to look, feel, touch, smell, and enjoy.

More than anything, people will remember the way you make them feel—and feeling great is what keeps people coming back. Ultimately, it's not about the clothes. It's about the connections we make.

> **My mission:** It's always been my goal to empower others. Over the years at Frox, I've connected with thousands of women. I've watched them transform right in front of my eyes as I teach them about fit and drape and how to best accentuate their unique body type. That feeling of empowerment though personal transformation has a ripple effect on how we see ourselves and also on how we're seen in the world. When you help a woman, everyone benefits: family, friends, and communities. It's the ultimate trickle down. My goal has been to help even more people. The story of how I wove together the threads of my life into a tapestry I'm proud of came to be in a book, *Behind the Button: Stories That Thread Us Together.* From my decades of time in the clothing and fashion industry, I've learned the value of creating your life to suit you and in choosing the clothing to suit your life—designing the best version of you inside and out.

My biggest challenge: My business made it through losing power for a week after Hurricane Sandy, the financial crisis of 2008, and 9/11. But nothing was more stressful than being forced to shut my doors during the COVID-19 pandemic. I watched some other business owners climb into a hole. I asked myself, "How can I serve and help my gals?" I had a website and was able to take online orders and personally deliver them.

We ramped up our very popular Frox-in-a-Box, where I open the boxes of our new, amazing merchandise live on social media. Going live was so much fun that I've continued doing it even after the store opened again.

The live videos were a party online, just as we had in the store when we were open. We started every live event by saying, "Grab your cocktail glass, and get ready for a great show." At the time, I had to model the clothes myself because everyone was safe at home. As it turns out, people liked it because I have a realistic body shape. As a bonus, I shared industry tips like the importance of the drape of clothing and how to care for fabrics.

How community helped my success: In addition to the Perkasie Town Improvement Association, I'm a member of several community groups, including a women's empowerment group called Sisters U, the Indian Valley Chamber of Commerce, and a book club. I call Perkasie the "little town that could." We all help each other and do what we can to enable all of us to thrive.

The relationships I've made are also a huge part of my success because I learn something from everyone, and I help others whenever I can. Our policy in the store is that if anyone is looking for a donation, the answer is always "yes." We have been fortunate to help hundreds of people and organizations.

My advice to other entrepreneurs: Believe in yourself and be absolutely authentic. Your clients want your unique perspective. You will attract more of those who share your vibe.

What I read and listen to: I'm currently reading Eckhart Tolle's *A New Earth: Awakening to Your Life's Purpose*. It has impacted everything I do in my personal and professional life. Other favorite authors and influencers include Jack Canfield, Lisa Nichols, and Brené Brown. I am a lifelong learner, always looking for a way to improve my world and myself.

At Insurance Chix, We Make Insurance Fun

Donna Hosfeld, owner of Hosfeld Insurance LLC, also known as Insurance Chix, in Alburtis

When I launched Hosfeld Insurance LLC in 1998, we were a pretty traditional agency. I wore power suits, and our website was navy and gray. I grew my business over the years, but there was one thing I wanted to change. I wanted my business to better represent who I was and what I brought to insurance—and that was a sense of comfort and fun.

I wanted to make insurance fun and interesting. Navy and gray were replaced with neon colors, and we traded our suits for jeans and tie-dyed shirts. I even tie-dyed my car. I also took on the name Insurance Chix and adopted a baby chick as our mascot, using it in the company logo and advertising.

Once I got people's attention, I worked on the teaching side of insurance. Rather than using dry terms and enigmatic acronyms that made my clients' eyes glaze over, I explained their policies in a way they could understand and appreciate. I've had clients tell me that no one had ever explained their insurance policy to them in a way they could understand before.

Taking this major turn was risky. Some people had doubts I could pull it off and questioned whether customers would take me seriously. I didn't want to lose all of the years of hard work I had put into building my agency, but after doing some soul searching, I thought it was the right thing to do.

The transition went perfectly. We stand out in the Lehigh Valley because of our marketing, and I was able to grow my business even more, expanding my staff to keep up with the new work coming in.

Another way we have fun and make a difference is through community involvement. We've held purse parties, hosted makeover events and summer concerts, and even collected children's knitted hats. We've raised thousands of dollars to help a variety of causes benefiting the local burn unit, the breast cancer assistance fund, animal rescue groups, and even efforts to abolish human trafficking.

I graduated from Kutztown University with a business degree and started in insurance claims. It was great training, but the culture of the company wasn't the right fit for me. I left and said I'd never work in insurance again. I got a position at Stabler Arena at Lehigh University and worked there for four years. I loved my job, but there was no chance to move up the ladder without moving from the Lehigh Valley.

Wanting more out of my career, I applied for a claims job at Erie Insurance, and from the first moment of my interview, I knew it was the job for me. I worked there for eight years and taught insurance courses for other employees.

When I was ready to move up, I applied for a position at Erie and was one of the top two people in the running to get it. The day I learned I didn't get the job crushed me. The person who interviewed me thought I'd be a better fit as an independent agent.

My agency is independent, which means I sell insurance from a variety of different insurance companies, but my primary carrier is Erie. The first two years were rough. I probably cried and kicked myself in the butt more than at any other time in my life. I worried it wouldn't pan out, but I trudged along, putting in long hours, until the day came when I could hire my first employee. Even though she only worked eight hours per week, having her on board made me sure we'd be okay. I had a team!

Reinventing Myself

Reinventing myself throughout the years—from swearing off insurance forever, loving the entertainment industry while at Stabler Arena, pivoting back again to insurance, opening my own agency, and then morphing into the fun, colorful agency we are today—is how I've reimagined success over and over throughout my career.

My agency's financial success is defined by numbers, like all businesses are. However, my overall "feeling of success" comes from enjoying my clients' lives with them. We join them to celebrate engagements, weddings, new home purchases, and children's births. Helping folks make wise financial choices and guiding them through the inevitable losses they'll experience is also incredibly rewarding. While car crashes, burned homes, and deaths are certainly not fun, they ARE a part of life. Being able to guide people through those times, assuring them they're not alone, and helping them when they are lost is when I can provide the value that an 800 number or website never will. I wholeheartedly believe in the value an independent agent provides to a client.

Our retention rate is something of which I am particularly proud. It's

My agency's financial success is defined by numbers, like all businesses must be. However, my overall "feeling of success" comes from enjoying my clients' lives with them.

in the mid-90th percentile, which is very high in any industry, particularly insurance. It means the service we're providing after the sale is valuable. It means the people who came on board *stayed* on board with us.

Insurance also gives me a chance to practice my first love. Since I was a kid, I've loved teaching. My career went in a different direction, but here's a fun fact: My job requires quite a bit of teaching. I teach my staff and my clients about how insurance works. Seeing someone's eyes light up because they finally "get it" is a rush!

- **How I schedule my time:** My days might start with some structure, but things can change in a heartbeat. Daily emails and voicemails can quickly change the direction of my day. We help our customers with claims, which isn't the case with all agencies. I might come in and learn that one of my insureds had a fender bender the night before. Or someone calls because the hail storm hit their neighborhood and their home doesn't look quite the same. One Sunday afternoon, I had a customer message me on Facebook to say her house was on fire, and she didn't know what to do. She was literally on the sidewalk watching the firefighters when I called her to let her know what would happen next. I drove to her home, hugged her, and walked her through the process. Within a few hours, she and her family (including pets) were checking into quarters that would be "home" for the next several months while repairs were completed. Delivering on "the promise" is when you know that what you're doing really matters.

- **What I read:** My favorite reads are biographies. Dolly Parton's new book, *Dolly Parton, Songteller: My Life in Lyrics*, is one I plan on reading. Reading how others got to where they are now is fascinating. No two paths are the same. But I love finding nuggets of inspiration that are part of everyone's story. I can't wait to read about everyone in this book!

My Personal Success Reimagined

Shelby Lawson, owner and designer of Lawson Accessories, in Bethlehem

I was born in a small town in South Carolina. Shortly after I was born, my dad enlisted in the military, and he moved to California. I rarely heard from him again. My only connection with my dad was hearing, "You must be Freeman's daughter! You look just like him."

My mom raised my older sister and me alone. But don't think it was a childhood of lack. My mom worked so hard that she bought her first home in her twenties—a three-bedroom rancher on an acre of land! Even with that success, my mom always reminded me that I could do even better. She told us to want more. She set the bar high for my image of success.

I enjoyed a happy childhood surrounded by extended family, including my paternal grandmother. She was a large woman, and I loved sewing muumuus for her, after learning how to sew in seventh grade home ec. Even though my dad lived clear across the county, his parents were a big part of my life.

Still as a child, I often wondered: *Where is my place in this world? Who I am? Who do I want to become? Why did my father leave? Did I inherit his "leaving" genes?*

When I was in my thirties, my husband and I moved to Pennsylvania, where our daughter was born. I worked for 17 years as a medical procedures scheduler, first for Lehigh Valley Health Network, then for St. Luke's University Health Network. I enjoyed my work. I felt I was living the successful life my mom had wanted for me. My plan was to work in that role until I retired.

But God had other plans.

Although I worked full-time, my hobby was sewing. It had been a part of my life since the seventh grade. In fall of 2016, I left St. Luke's and opened Lawson Accessories, selling my handmade table runners and other accents.

Today, my customers are women ranging from their twenties to their over-seventies. Their ages vary, but they all have one thing in common: They want to feel beautiful. I want them to feel unique and special. My goal is to give every woman who walks into my store a bit of joy.

I often talk with my customers in the Victorian-themed sitting area of my store. We sip tea—or wine if it's that sort of talk. We live in a go-go-go society. When you come to Lawson Accessories, be prepared to stay awhile!

When I was 40 years old, my husband said something out of the blue: "You need to forgive your father." I didn't know where that came from! I hadn't had any contact with my father, nor did I really miss his presence in my life. I think that maybe I was presenting something to my husband that I couldn't see myself.

I took pen in hand and wrote my dad a letter, including, "I forgive you for not being there." I mailed the letter to my half-brother who still lives in South Carolina, asking him to mail it to our dad. I don't know if he did. I know I never heard back.

But the instant I put that letter in my mailbox, a weight lifted from my spirit. I felt like I was floating as I walked back inside my house.

I can move on with my life, I thought. *I don't need my dad in it. I've done my part. I've forgiven him.* Ready to wash my hands of it all, I set about getting back to living my life.

Fast forward to a rainy Wednesday in 2019. My shop was closed. Still wearing my pjs, I settled into my couch to enjoy a cup of coffee before doing some sewing in my workshop. Out of nowhere, I heard, "Reach out to your dad." It was not my imagination; I heard it out loud!

My dad was now 82 years old. I didn't know anything about him—not even where he lived. I turned to Facebook: today's Yellow Pages. *Why would an 82-year-old have a Facebook page?* I wondered.

But he did! For several hours, I scrolled through images of my dad—looking so much like me. I saw his wife, the other sons I had heard he had, his extended family, and photos of the church and congregation he ministered. I also saw a young woman and wondered who she was. I messaged her: "I think we're related."

The next day, my phone rang. I recognized a California area code.

"Hi! This is Alexis," said the voice at the other end of the line. "How are you?"

As we talked, I realized I was talking to my younger sister. I gave her the time and space to realize this herself. When she did, she cried. "All my life, I wanted a sister," she said.

Alexis offered to share my phone number with our dad. A few days later, I was at my shop when the phone rang. I knew instinctively it was him, so I said, "This is Shelby. Who's calling?"

"Freeman. Your father," he said.

"Well, well, well," I replied.

After that, my dad began his story from nearly the beginning—the day he left South Carolina. He talked for an hour while I was in the shop. He talked for another hour while I drove home on Route 22. I walked in the house, looked at my husband, pointed to my phone, and mouthed, "My daddy." For another hour, my husband held my hand as I listened to my dad talk. As I listened, the feeling of forgiveness seeped deeper into my soul.

Alexis and I made plans to meet in person in Las Vegas where serendipitously both she and my husband had work conferences. I'll never forget how I felt when I saw her for the first time, gliding down an escalator toward me. As we connected, she kept staring at me and touching my face.

"You look just like Daddy, but with lipstick on," she exclaimed. I immediately embraced her as my sister.

Today, my father and I, and Alexis and I, are building upon our new relationships. The changes in my life after truly forgiving my dad have been remarkable. Once you answer the questions you've had, heal the pain, and forgive, it wipes away the unpleasantness. I never thought I would feel this way; I thought I would carry my longing and hurt to my grave. In order to grow and move on, I needed to forgive.

At the time when I reconnected with my dad, my business at Lawson Accessories was steady. But once I started my forgiveness journey, doors started to open all around me. I wanted to expand my store, so I asked my landlord about renting the space next to me. I discovered the military recruitment center had just given notice to move, and the space opened up for me. I went to the Allentown Art Museum with an idea to hold a fashion show there. In 2020, *Lehigh Valley Style* called me for an interview. So did PBS. I received a Lehigh Valley Business Award as a Game Changer.

One after another, opportunities came. So much was going on it made me want to go deeper in my forgiveness with my father. Even bigger and better things began to happen. When you do the right thing, good things happen to you.

My feelings about success were completely reimagined for me when I forgave my father. I'm enjoying success in a field that I had never imagined I would be a part of. I'm still not where I want to be—but I will be. My daughter graduated from college and is setting out on her own journey, freeing me to create and do what I please. I know there are no limitations on my success because of my act of forgiveness.

I Took a Winding Path from Counselor to Entrepreneur and Now Mentor

Erin Miller, photographer, counselor, mentor,
owner of Erin Joyce Co., author of *Motherhood Stripped*,
and host of the podcast *Same Boat Huddle*

S ome people believe success is choosing a career path at 18 and retiring from it at 65. That is one way to be successful, but I've taken a different, more fluid, journey.

I began my career with a counseling degree and worked as an elementary school counselor. It was an amazing job that I didn't anticipate leaving. But my school district underwent a massive restructuring that made public education a more difficult space for me to work, the school was an hour away from home, and I became pregnant with my daughter. At a younger age, I had romanticized dropping my child off at daycare and working full-time, but when the time came, I realized how much time I wouldn't be able to see my daughter.

I was a very good counselor, but that didn't mean it was my purpose in life. I chose to leave my job.

For as long as I can remember, I've enjoyed photography. My childhood pictures show me always with a camera in my hand. I learned photography on film in high school and continued photography as a hobby with a digital camera after graduate school.

Word got around among my family and friends that I had a passion for taking pictures. I started a 365 project photo journal and posted a picture online every day. I also started taking pictures of my friends' kids. Photography soon became a business that grew organically.

A large part of the success of my photography business had to do with my counseling background. Counselors have a louder sixth sense to feel out how people are doing and feeling. I'm intuitively connected to my clients as I photograph them and shoot based on their feelings and emotions. If a couple isn't connecting emotionally in a pose, I move them out of it and into something else. My clients tell me how easy and fun their photo shoots are, even on their wedding day when emotions of excitement and stress can reach a peak.

But as my business was booming, I was headed for burnout. I hustled and worked my tail off to try to replace the salary I left in counseling. I did, and then I kept going—all while juggling being a mom to an infant and a toddler. I wasn't eating or sleeping enough, and I was missing out on the joys of life.

My anxiety grew until I suffered from a severe, debilitating anxiety attack that put me in urgent care.

It was a long climb out, but therapy and consulting with a hormonal nutritionist to figure out how to feed my body after recently giving birth guided me back to health and success. Later, I also hired a life coach, who helped even more. Like a trainer at a gym, my life coach helped me get stronger as a person and determine the steps I wanted to take in my career. I had felt alone at the beginning of my journey, but I soon realized that many women are in the same boat, feeling anxiety and being overwhelmed.

My Next Step

It was time for my next step: to transform my career and become a mentor, coach, and author. I help women move out of feeling that they're only surviving to feeling expansive, joyful and aligned in life.

Currently, I'm doing both photography and coaching, but I'm letting intuition guide me as I move forward. I'm achieving success based on how I feel rather than having a preconceived idea of how much money I should be making. This mindset is bringing me even more prosperity.

- **How I view success:** I believe we, as a society, view success in too strict of a box. We've been taught that if you make a certain amount of money, you're successful—even if you're miserable or unhealthy. I believe success means living with purpose and joy.

- **How daily photos impact my life:** It's been about eight years since I started posting daily with the 365 project photo journal, and I still do it, although I've moved from posting to a blog to social media. I find it helps with personal development. Looking back at the pictures from the year helps me process my days and life lessons.

- **How I set my schedule:** I take a different approach to scheduling my days. I set my schedule based on a 28-day cycle in order to honor my

I'm achieving success based on how I feel rather than having a preconceived idea of how much money I should be making. This mindset is bringing me even more prosperity.

body and energy levels. Women tend to have a couple of weeks when we're flooded with creativity, energy, and new ideas. Those are the days when I'm most productive and when I'll schedule phone calls, meetings, and photo shoots.

Women also experience several days where we take inventory, go into an inward state, and analyze our lives. It's a time when we can become prone to being moody and labeled as "hormonal." These can be some of the most productive days and weeks for a woman if we are aware and in sync with our bodies. On those days, I try to avoid scheduling too much. When I do have commitments, I sandwich them with self-care, getting rest, and deep cleaning around the house. If I try to power through during the phases when I need more rest, it will feel like I'm walking through quicksand, and later, when I should have more energy, I'll be depleted. I also depend on good sleep and a morning routine that includes meditation and journaling.

What I listen to: I often listen to podcasts, such as *Mom Is in Control, Earn Your Happy,* and *EmpowerHER*. I also listen to music for a brain break.

I Left the Corporate World, Got Into the Sign Business, and Made a Mark in the Lehigh Valley

Steve Gingras, president of Valley Wide Signs and Graphics in Allentown, JHM Signs in New Jersey, and Sign Shop of the Poconos in Allentown

Anyone who strolls down Bethlehem's Main Street will likely notice a piece of my company's work. Above the entrance to the bar and grill Corked is a sign we made based on the restaurant's logo, which has something unique: The "E" is in the shape of a corkscrew.

When I saw the logo, I knew it would take some research and creativity to figure out how to make it into a sign. I ultimately found exhaust pipes from an aircraft manufacturing company that fit the bill perfectly. That's part of the fun of my job.

I'm trained as a chemical engineer, and I spent 26 years in the corporate world as an executive for a couple of companies, starting with Air Products and moving on to another company where I managed their business throughout the Americas.

But from 2008 to 2010, the economy tanked, and my job was eliminated. There were no comparable jobs in the Lehigh Valley, given the economy. I didn't want to move my family out of the area, so I made a call to a business broker to look into options for buying a business.

In 2010, I bought Valley Wide Signs and Graphics, and in 2018, I expanded the business by buying two more companies, JHM Signs in New Jersey and Sign Shop of the Poconos here in Pennsylvania. They serve as sister companies to Valley Wide Signs.

The three companies complement each other because they each focus on a

different aspect of the sign business. Valley Wide Signs creates and assembles signs, the Sign Shop of the Poconos installs signs, and JHM Signs installs and services signs, repairing them when lights go out or making adjustments when needed, as well as doing vehicle wraps. That's a very simplified summary of each company, but there is a lot of synergy among the three of them.

That allowed us to take on national customers, such as Starbucks, that have their signs made outside of the Lehigh Valley but need someone local to do the installation or to service them.

Growing My Business

Having an engineer's mind helps in my business because I take a logical approach to my work. I use analysis in business decisions, such as whether to buy a new piece of equipment or to repair what we already have. The purchases I've made have allowed Valley Wide Signs to produce prototypes more quickly and have given us greater capabilities to grow.

Our geographic reach has also expanded through our acquisitions. We have local clients with locations in other states. Halloween City, for example, has pop-up stores in several states, and we install the signs for about 70 of their locations along the East Coast from New Hampshire to South Carolina. B. Braun, another client, hired us to make several custom signs and asked us to ship them to their facility in California and install them.

I went from working for companies with hundreds or thousands of employees to running three companies with 15 employees. It was a completely unexpected change to my career, but one I'm happy I made. I've grown Valley Wide Signs' revenue to about double where it was at the time of the purchase. We're the largest independent full-service sign company in the Lehigh Valley region.

The most satisfying part of owning my businesses is the sense of accomplishment I get from driving around and seeing signs we've made and installed all over the Lehigh Valley. I always point them out to my wife and daughter—much to their annoyance. It's good to see what we've created and to know my signs will be up for years.

■ **How I differentiate my business:** After I bought Valley Wide Signs, I realized there was room to focus more on meeting our customers' needs after the initial sale to generate more repeat business. I focused on making our customers ecstatic about our services. As a result of this commitment, the average sale to our customers grew dramatically.

We've also expanded our product offerings by buying new equipment.

The most satisfying part of owning my businesses is the sense of accomplishment I get from driving around and seeing signs we've made and installed all over the Lehigh Valley.

The combination of equipment we have isn't common among companies in the Lehigh Valley, so that means we can turn projects around and provide prototypes and samples to our customers more quickly. In addition to customized one-of-a-kind signs, we create banners, decals, and vehicle graphics.

Good people are key: I originally bought a company in an industry I didn't know much about, but it had a great general manager and team of employees, which were invaluable. This was also true of the two more recent acquisitions. They both have very strong managers and great people. My philosophy is to make sure you have good people, give them the tools they need, and get out of the way.

One of my secrets to success: I've always believed, "The secret is: There are no secrets," at least in my industry. Rather than giving competitors the cold shoulder, I meet with them and take them through my shop. I know there's nothing a competitor will learn by going through the shop that will change what we do or what they do. But creating a relationship means that if I'm in a jam, I can make a call and have them make something for me. I'll do the same for them. I got to know JHM Signs and Sign Shop of the Poconos this way, which was the primary reason I ended up buying them.

What I read: It fascinates me to look at something and think, *How will we make this?* So, I spend a lot of time researching how things are put together. We'll get a photo or a spec of a sign from a potential customer, and I'll go to work doing research into how it's made. We might not end up getting that specific job, but I learned something new, and that has a lot of ramifications for what we can do in the future.

During my corporate days, I enjoyed reading Jim Collins's *Good to Great* and Patrick Lencioni's books on leadership. For pleasure reading, I've always enjoyed Tom Clancy's original works.

I Restore Worn, Tattered, Broken-Down Properties to Their Former Glory—And Bring Relief to Families

Pawl Good, owner of Good Community Properties in Whitehall

W e've all seen houses that at one point are grand and striking, but fall into disarray over the years. I watched it happen to a house on my street when I was a kid. As it transformed from a beautiful home to an ugly property that was falling apart, I wondered, *What's going on with that house?*

It was a burning question in my mind, even as a kid. Because my family moved often for my dad's job, I didn't stay long enough to get the answer. Still, I found myself drawn to old houses that needed TLC.

It's part of what led me to start Good Community Properties about six years ago. Again, a house on my street piqued my interest. It was a new age home, and the elderly couple who lived there passed away. There were no heirs to reclaim the home, and property back taxes were the only debt accumulating on it. It took four and a half years for the house to go up on tax auction. I didn't purchase it, but I watched it through the entire process of it sitting empty and getting uglier to being transformed to its previous glory. I finally had one explanation for how houses fall into shambles.

I also learned that sometimes houses are reflections of the hard times their owners are going through. My company specializes in buying distressed properties and working with sellers who can't get a sale through the traditional real estate route. Unwanted, "problem" properties are right up my alley. When I breathe life and hope into a situation where a family has fallen on hard times, I'm doing what I set out to do.

Here's one example: During my company's second year in business, an elderly man responded to my direct mail marketing. He was guarded at first

about his intentions for calling, like most people are when they're struggling with something. He was living alone in his home of 55 years, and his family had left him behind and forgotten. He was no longer able to care for and maintain the home.

Through months of conversations, meetings, and research, I helped him find an assisted living facility he liked. We downsized his belongings, contacted his remaining heirs, and helped him move. He was giddy with excitement about the positive changes in his life.

I bought the house, cleaned it out, and sent off several family pieces to out-of-state relatives. The 55-year-old home had never been renovated, and many of the walls had never even been repainted. We brought it back to its original shine with new paint, carpeting, and flooring.

That's what I love to do—to take something that's worn, tattered, and beaten down and bring it back to life. In the case of this house, I still keep in touch with the original owner. I sent him photos and videos of the process as we transformed the property.

The majority of our projects aren't this dramatic, but it's why I have a passion for real estate. I love showing people who can't see the light at the end of the tunnel that we can figure this out.

Our Other Areas of Growth

There's another facet to my business. We also partner with investors who want to build wealth through real estate, whether they want to be active or passive participants. We pay a pretty healthy interest rate on their investment, which is secured and protected by the real estate itself.

- **Reimagining success is ongoing for me:** My vision of the future of my company is constantly evolving and changing. Every quarter and every year, I consider what may be the company's shortcomings and look for ideas I can implement to get to my goals.

- **What propels my success:** I worked in the logistics and supply chain business before starting my company, first in the Lehigh Valley and then in California. I started as a forklift manager and rose up through

When I breathe life and hope into a situation where a family has fallen on hard times, I'm doing what I set out to do.

My vision of the future of my company is constantly evolving and changing. Every quarter and every year, I consider what may be the company's shortcomings and look for ideas I can implement to get to my goals.

the ranks from there—faster than most people. Then and now, I ask a lot of *why* questions: Why am I doing something this way? Why can't I get contractors to show up on time? They're important questions because they force me to find solutions.

■ **How I define success:** It's pretty simple: hard work, grit, determination—and the ability to not accept failure as an option. You're going to fail. There's no question about it. How many times are you willing to fail to get it right? That's the goal; that's the success. It's also about asking tough questions of yourself and being willing to accept critical feedback when you need to.

■ **The best advice I've ever gotten:** "Take action." I'm an analytical guy and can spend a year trying to analyze what I want to do. I spent two to three years doing research on how to flip houses before doing it. When I finally did get a property, I learned more in six months than in years of research.

■ **How I set my schedule:** I have "shiny object syndrome" like nobody's business. There's no real structure to my day, but I know what I want to accomplish.

■ **What I read and listen to:** I'm currently reading *Miracle Morning Millionaires: What the Wealthy Do Before 8 AM That Will Make You Rich* by Hal Elrod, David Osborn, and others. I also recently finished for the fourth time the fantastic negotiation book *Never Split the Difference: Negotiating As If Your Life Depended On It* by Chris Voss.

I also listen to Don Costa's *Flip Talk*, Les Brown's *Greatness Radio*, and *The Tony Robbins Podcast*.

In Real Estate, There's a Solution to Everything— If You Get Creative

Carol Landis-Pierce, SRS, Realtor with Coldwell Banker Hearthside
in Allentown and a member of the Cliff Lewis Experience,
a leading real estate team in the Lehigh Valley

When I joined the world of real estate more than 12 years ago, it was an unexpected turn in a career that I continued to re-envision as I grew and honed my skills—and being a problem-solver was key to reaching new heights.

My career began in the typing pool at Bethlehem Steel. We typed letters that people throughout the office had hand-written or dictated. I went home crying every day because I hated being confined to a desk for eight hours. My job isn't satisfying unless I'm interacting with other people. I stuck it out and moved on to very rewarding positions at Bethlehem Steel, eventually managing the personal computing command center. We were the help line during the time when personal computers were being used for the first time, so we got staff members out of technology crises.

I moved on from Bethlehem Steel and did corporate training sales for a tech company, where I rose to become the number one sales rep in the country with a client base in the Lehigh Valley.

Real estate wasn't on my radar until my daughter called me as she was finishing college and said, "Mom, we need to get into real estate." I told her to put a plan together, and we purchased a rental property in Allentown, which we still have today. She enjoyed the experience so much that she became a real estate agent.

Two years later, when I became weary of the travel my job required and the ups and downs of corporate budgets, I decided to try something new and joined my daughter at Coldwell Banker. And about three years ago, I joined the Cliff Lewis Experience, which makes me a member of one of the leading real estate teams in the Lehigh Valley.

My Success Strategy

A key to my success in every stage of my career has been problem-solving. I like putting together solutions. That means I have a goal of giving my clients a good experience when they're buying a home, whether they're first-time homebuyers, they're downsizing, or they're upsizing.

It starts at the very beginning of the process when my clients are looking for a lender. I work with a number of lenders and pair my clients with a lender with whom I think they'll work well.

Problem-solving also comes into play when structuring a deal. I learned from my daughter the importance of thoroughly understanding contracts. In Pennsylvania, we use standard contracts, but there are many of them, so I have to understand the ones I use regularly, and I have to be familiar with the add-ons clients might choose to tack on to the standard agreement.

We're not lawyers, but having a thorough command of what we're getting our clients into and how to use contracts is vital to my business. Plus, knowing the contracts inside and out means I can get creative when structuring deals that make it more likely my clients will get what they want out of the purchase.

Being a problem-solver and having command over the contracts helped me get through one of the most complex years of all my time doing real estate, and that was 2020. Inventory was very low, and demand was very high. We had to manage during a pandemic with changing rules about which businesses were considered essential and which businesses needed to shut down. Early in the year, when real estate wasn't considered an essential business, we had clients make offers on houses they hadn't even seen.

Once real estate agents could get back to work full-time, many of my clients had to submit 5 to 10 offers before one would be accepted. Because it was a seller's market, deals in which the buyers asked the sellers to assist with closing costs were declined. I get to know people emotionally, and I experience the disappointment along with them when things don't go their way.

I also had some big wins during the year. One of my clients made one of 17 offers on a house—and was accepted. It took getting creative with the terms of the agreement to get the sale. We did everything we could to stand out from other buyers, including using flexible terms and a larger deposit to get the deal.

Buying a home is one of the biggest financial decisions in life, and I do everything I can to make my clients happy.

Being a problem-solver and having command over the contracts helped me get through one of the most complex years of all my time doing real estate.

What I love about real estate: Real estate might look easy, but it's not necessarily a quick start or an immediate money maker. It's not quite how it looks on HGTV, where you go out and see three houses and make an offer. It takes a lot of work, and it may take up to six months to start making money. On the plus side: Real estate and sales is one career where what you do directly affects the money you make. I have more control over my salary than in any other industry. Working more and working smarter pays off.

How I structure my time: I live by my calendar, and no two days are the same. I use Google, which is on my laptop and connected to my phone, and my calendar is shared with other people in my office and my family so they can see where I am and what I'm doing.

What I read and listen to: I have a new habit of following what's going on politically. I also like to listen to Christian music.

Creating a New Category of Landscaping Business Meant a Change in Philosophy

Joshua Gillow, owner of MasterPLAN Outdoor Living and
YesExpress, and a buy-and-hold real estate investor

Personality is personified in business. It's a principle I've learned as a serial entrepreneur and one I live by as the owner of the outdoor design/build company MasterPLAN Outdoor Living and the sales training program YesExpress, which helps landscape design/build professionals grow their businesses in smart and efficient ways.

My mother opened a garden center when I was five years old, and I got my start in business as a kid when I collected cool rocks in the nearby fields and sold them at her store. Later, I studied architecture and technology and merged what I knew about gardening and landscaping with the design world to start a landscaping company with my brother and father.

Venturing Out on My Own

Then, nine years ago, I branched out on my own to do something truly unique. I launched MasterPLAN to help clients seamlessly merge their indoor and outdoor spaces. We take a holistic design approach so that their outdoor space looks like it was done with the same brushstroke as the rest of the property. That philosophy adds incredible beauty to the property as a whole, and it also adds the best comfort and return on investment.

We created a new category of landscaping business that was much more than a "chuck in a truck" company. In order to get the new company where we wanted—bringing massive impact to people's lives by creating amazing outdoor living spaces that bring family and friends closer together—I had to re-evaluate my approach to business. It took a complete change in my philosophy and my thinking in every aspect of my life, including a lot of personal growth.

This year, I began the sales program YesExpress to share what I've learned

over the past 24 years in the trenches with others in my industry. My goal is to empower my students with tried-and-true sales strategies (specifically for our industry) that will help them take their businesses to the next level, boost their closing rates, and build a wickedly profitable business.

Here are some of the concepts I learned to propel my business to new heights that can help my students do the same for their companies.

- **I stopped thinking about my competition.** If you chase your competition, you're always following. I don't. I think about what I did yesterday and ask myself, "What can I do today to get two millimeters closer to my goal?"

  The two-millimeter rule is a concept I picked up from following life coach Tony Robbins. In my business, one way I push myself two millimeters is through client experience, such as handling all of the documents so clients don't have to get their own permits.

  I also apply the concept to every aspect of my life, from my health and fitness to my family life and lifestyle. There are 100 ways to push yourself toward your goals.

- **I started to love making bad decisions.** People tend to sit on the edge of making a decision because they're worried about failing. But failure means you're out of your comfort zone and you're moving forward. If I make a wrong decision, I'll learn pretty quickly and be wiser next time. People who are successful have had the guts to spend at least 10,000 hours screwing up—and that's what makes them so good at what they do. You miss out on 100 percent of the opportunities you don't pursue.

- **I became good at setting goals.** For years, I did what most people do: I set goals in January and realized months later that I hadn't achieved them. My goals weren't wired with enough of the "why." It was time to ask myself, why do I want to achieve this?

  I started creating goals for my business for the next one, three, five, and 10 years. I put them on paper to make them more substantial and help hold me accountable to them. And then I review them weekly or monthly to make sure I'm on track.

  Today, I don't always hit my goals at the exact time I had hoped, but I know every step in the right direction helps get me closer. Defining what I want the future to look like is the critical piece. It creates momentum.

- **I learn from mentors.** Mentors have had a huge impact on my career. It makes sense to partner with coaches and mentors who have already been down the path you're treading and learn from their successes and mistakes. My first mentors were my parents, and I've also sought out other coaches and mentors to teach me different perspectives of my business, including sales.

Another mentor who changed my life is Tony Robbins. In live events, which I've attended, he taught me how to be the best version of myself.

I set personal goals that push me physically and mentally. When I was around 38, my son came home from an American Ninja Warrior–themed birthday party and told me he thought I would like it. American Ninja Warriors reach the height of fitness and strength to compete in obstacle courses. I had never been to a gym and considered my work my exercise. But I thought about how I wanted to control my own fate, and this could be one way to do that. After training with a coach, I decided I really liked it and started to compete.

Competing wasn't only about gaining strength. It was also about focus and being disciplined with my diet. I cut out sugar, caffeine, and most gluten. I also fast every once in a while. I started out fasting for 18 hours, and then I was challenged to push it further, so I fasted for 36 hours and later did it for 60 hours. It helps turn off what I call my "monkey brain" that tells me I can't do something.

I've even tried out for the American Ninja Warrior television show three times. I was able to get to the test course twice but haven't gotten on TV—yet. I'm going to keep trying until I get a yes.

What I read:

- *The Big Five for Life* by John Strelecky, an inspirational book about how to be a leader in every aspect of your life.

- *Can't Hurt Me: Master Your Mind and Defy the Odds* by David Goggins, which tells the amazing story of the author's life of overcoming adversity and how all of us are capable of pushing ourselves further than we imagined.

- *Never Split the Difference: Negotiating As If Your Life Depended on It* by Chris Voss, in which a career hostage negotiator explains how to handle the daily negotiations we find ourselves in every day.

- *Atlas Shrugged* by Ayn Rand, a classic novel about philosophy and business.

My Insurance Agency's Niche in the Lehigh Valley Is the Underserved Multicultural Market

Dave Lin, owner and principal agent of Linwood Forest Insurance Group in Whitehall and real estate investor

I have a goal of retiring young, and I'm getting there through some unique ways. I'm the only Chinese-speaking property and casualty insurance agent in the Lehigh Valley, and we also have a Spanish-speaking agent on staff. This allows us to serve the multicultural market in the area that was previously lacking.

I've been in the insurance industry since 2011 and started Linwood Forest Insurance Group in 2014. No one grows up wanting to be an insurance agent. The majority of people fall into the industry. I enjoy helping people secure their assets: homes, autos, and businesses. I also work as the first point of contact in the event of a loss so my clients feel they have someone on their side—me.

As an independent agent, I represent multiple insurance companies. If a particular company's policy doesn't fit one of my client's situations, I can offer them other choices. This allows my agency to focus on providing the right coverage at the right price for my clients, resulting in long-term client retention.

In the insurance industry, new agencies tend to fail at a rate of 80 percent in the first three years. My ability to grow and beat these odds is in large part because I am able to leverage my personal strengths. I was born in Fujian, China, and I speak three dialects of Chinese. The Lehigh Valley has more than 1,000 Chinese-American households, and I focus my skill set on nurturing those relationships. Many of these clients were working with non-Chinese-speaking agents in the past and were unable to communicate their needs appropriately in their native dialect. I began by sending direct mailers to these households, outlining why I would be able to better help them with my background and abilities.

Building Successful Relationships

I have been building a relationship network with Realtors and mortgage groups to generate tertiary lead sources to keep my agency moving forward organically. One of the ways I give back to these partnerships is by providing a company branded key for them to use with their clients for photos at closing. I have received excellent feedback from this and continue to get referrals from other members of their professional community as well. Due to the success from this, I have been able to scale back direct marketing and continue to build my centers of influence.

My main focus is to retain my clientele. To do this, I have a dedicated service agent who focuses on providing quick solutions and cross selling additional lines of insurance to keep them from working with other agents.

My other line of business is focused on real estate investing, in particular, hard money lending. Due to time constraints from my insurance agency, I don't have time to manage and oversee a group of contractors running home remodels as people picture when they think of real estate investing. Instead, I lend money to other real estate investors at higher than normal interest rates due to barriers they face with traditional lending sources. These primarily consist of credit rating issues or timing issues with banks requiring longer tails for mortgage appraisal, applications and credit checks.

I have a goal of retiring in 15 years, by the age of 50—a couple of years earlier if things go better. I call myself the laziest hard-working person I know. I'm working harder now so I can be lazy in the future.

A common challenge in my business: Hiring new employees.

My main focus is to retain my clientele. To do this, I have a dedicated service agent who focuses on providing quick solutions and cross selling additional lines of insurance to keep them from working with other agents.

I call myself the laziest hard-working person I know. I'm working harder now so I can be lazy in the future.

My agency is growing quickly. I have three staff members, and I'm looking to hire another person so I can focus on building my business further. If you know of anyone, send them my way! The largest issue in hiring young people into this industry is that insurance has been marketed as a commodity, leaving a lot of what we do an unknown. The majority of people who really understand the benefit and niche of an insurance agency outside the industry are professionals who utilize us to manage their risks and protect their assets.

My background in the Navy: I served four years in the U.S. Navy, and that helped establish my work ethic and mold my personality to become someone who is driven, completing all the goals I put into motion.

My Best: Building My Own Architecture Firm from the Ground Up

Samantha Ciotti Falcone, AIA, LEED AP,
owner of SCF Architecture, LLC

If you've ever admired the beautiful details of a home or building, you can thank the architect for those aesthetic features. While developer-led projects focus on efficiency and tend to result in a box, architects are often responsible for what makes buildings special.

There's an office/apartment building in downtown Allentown with a gorgeous green wall of plants in the lobby that can be seen from the street. That's the type of creativity architects bring to a project, and it's something I always look to add in my work.

I helped Univest develop their bank branch prototype. The old branch design had curved windows, so I included a curved wall in the design of the lobby to soften the rigid bank model. We added fresh, modern lighting, a curved couch, and rounded furniture. We included the bank's media wall along the curve to bring attention to a digital monitor displaying marketing messages.

Architects often get pushback from contractors and developers who are most concerned about the budget and efficiency. The contractor on the Univest project tried to "value engineer" the curved wall out of the design, but it ultimately remained. I'm glad because it adds interest when you walk into the bank's branches—that special something that draws your attention and makes the space feel different than "vanilla" retail space.

Even when I have a box to work with, I find ways to make a project special. I worked on plans for the Bethany Church in Macungie. It was a pre-engineered, metal building, but I added multi-level ceiling "clouds" (suspended ceiling grids with edges) to the lobby that took away the warehouse feel of the vast, open lobby space and made it a pleasing place for people to gather. Their worship space needed to feel like a church for services, but it had

to also serve as a gym for youth events and function well for both activities. Acoustical panels plus durable, classic-feeling finishes like wood-grained commercial vinyl plank flooring and black ceiling paint that makes the ceiling-mounted basketball nets disappear did the trick.

Architecture is in my blood, as my uncle was trained as an architect and my grandfather was a stone carver who worked on some of the most iconic churches and buildings in New York City. My parents encouraged my art "habit," and my school notebooks were always filled with doodles and sketches. However, I didn't think much about making architecture a career until I was in high school. I had been looking into art schools for college when I met with a guidance counselor and discovered architecture would be a wonderful career choice because it combined all of my favorite subjects in school: art, science, history, and math.

With good grades and a lot of hard work, I was admitted to the competitive Carnegie Mellon University architecture department in Pittsburgh. It's a tough program, but once I decided I wanted to do this, I put my heart into it, and it was the perfect fit.

During college, I saw myself becoming my own boss one day. But during my summers off from college and after graduating, I started working for architecture firms—in the Lehigh Valley and in Pittsburgh—and realized it was nice to do the fun parts of being an architect without worrying about doing payroll, dealing with insurance, and completing other business tasks. For one firm, I completed a lot of church projects, and I gained experience working on a shoestring budget and getting the most bang for the buck out of the construction budget.

Time for Reinvention

My view changed, though, after the financial crisis in 2008 and subsequent recession. It led to changes at the firm I was working at that I didn't agree with, and I decided it was time to invest in something I believed in. I made the leap and founded my own architecture firm, promising not to repeat some of the things I had observed in other firms I had worked for.

I started by working on any projects I could find and providing architectural services to other architecture firms, helping them in their crunch times and forming a referral source. I also reached out to real estate agents and contractors who had commercial clients. Through my professional networking, I know architects in almost every firm in the Lehigh Valley, and they started referring work to me that was too small for their larger companies. One project turned into six, and my company has been growing since then. Today I have a small staff, and we work with residential and commercial clients. We do projects that range anywhere from a front porch renovation or residential addition to a $5 million new commercial building. I couldn't do what I do without the help of my amazing staff.

I'm also a LEED Accredited Professional, which means my designs and the materials I specify put less stress on the environment. We take advantage of solar angles and shade when designing homes and buildings, and we use non-toxic materials wherever possible. Ultimately, happy clients are my goal and my success story.

How I sharpened my leadership skills: In high school, participating in marching band helped me learn some leadership skills and gave me confidence to present myself in public. Later, in college, I joined the American Institute of Architecture Students and soon became chapter president and went on to become one of their national directors. The experience and training this organization gave me has been an invaluable tool and has given me a passion for organizational planning and leadership that has helped me in so many ways throughout my adult life.

My biggest challenge: Self-doubt and confidence are things every leader struggles with. When I share these issues with people, they're amazed because I carry myself with confidence and present myself well. But sometimes, behind the scenes, the ducks aren't always in a nice, neat row. They're flying off in every direction.

My tips for budding entrepreneurs: Take time to understand your skill set and turn to others to fill in the gaps. No one person can be great at everything. Believe in yourself and try not to compare yourself to your peers. You're doing amazing things in your own way.

How I schedule my day: I'm not an organized, linear thinker, so every day is different for me. I have about 15 different things on my mind at any one time. I keep a running list of tasks to do before I leave the office, and I push myself to "eat the frogs," which means do the things I've been avoiding first so I can get to the rest of my goals. The mental energy wasted on those less pleasant tasks takes away from everything else.

What I listen to: I'm a self-help addict, and I'm always trying to improve something, so I listen to the *Business of Architecture* podcasts, business improvement seminars, and continuing education webinars often. Someone once told me, "Learn something new every day."

Chasing the Doggie Dream: Taking Care of Dogs Is My Passion and My Business

Rayne Reitnauer, CVT, owner Cold Nose Lodge, which offers doggie daycare, training, luxury dog boarding, grooming, and other services in Alburtis

I noticed when I volunteered at local animal rescue groups several years ago that many of the dogs abandoned at shelters had common issues, such as jumping and biting, all of which could have been resolved if they had been properly trained as puppies. This was the spark that inspired me to open my own dog training and day care center.

But first I wanted education. I worked toward a veterinary technician degree and sought additional training on how dogs learn. My education led me to my next revelation: In training dogs, I would use only positive reinforcement and redirection. Any punishments would be in the form of taking away a potential reward, such as my attention, a toy, or play time (a time out).

Prong collars, choke chains, and other tools that use negative reinforcement are often recommended by trainers. They're an easy fix for something like pulling during walks. In fact, at the direction of my trainer, I used a choke chain on my dog myself when I was in my early 20s.

But as Maya Angelou said, "When you know better, you do better." I now know better. I know that dogs absolutely can become happy, well-behaved members of the family without resorting to behavior enforcement tools that cause them pain or stress.

I also understand that it's easy to make mistakes even when you have the best of intentions—because I've been there. When my husband and I were engaged, we adopted a puppy, Jack. We took Jack to puppy class and thought things were going well, but as he matured, he became reactive to other dogs. Our solution was to avoid other dogs.

What I know now is that we failed to socialize Jack enough as a puppy. We

Pictured with "Trace" Beagle/Staffordshire/Boxer mix

never got Jack to the point where he was able to go back to day care or greet other dogs up close, but with work we could take him camping and for walks. I continued working with Jack, and fortunately his behavior improved until he was the perfect dog during his last year of life.

I bring this experience, knowledge, patience, and care to every dog who comes to Cold Nose Lodge. My goal is to build a trusting, joyful, rewarding relationship between people and their dogs, to make living with them, walking them, and taking them out and about a joy.

I also never want a dog to feel any anxiety or distress coming to the Lodge. For instance, if a dog comes in for a nail trim and is extremely stressed, we don't do the trim that day. Some dogs may need medication to calm them, and others may even need to be anesthetized for a good trim. One of my client's dogs likes to do a handstand during the trim, and we allow it. If a dog prefers a particular member of our staff, we schedule their visit accordingly. We use the same scheduling model for baths, daycare, and boarding.

I'm happy to say we've made dog owners' and their pets' lives better. Some have told us that if they didn't have the option to use our daycare, they wouldn't be able to keep their high-energy dog. Dogs get plenty of exercise and playtime here. We have two large indoor playrooms and three outside yards with climbers and bone-shaped pools. We also blow bubbles and play follow the leader for additional enrichment. The dogs settle down for nap time around noon.

One of My Greatest Successes

We can even say we've saved a marriage! One of our clients told us his marriage was becoming strained because he didn't trust any facility to board his dog. He was missing out on trips with his wife to visit her family as a result. Once he tried our daycare and his dog loved it, he ended up feeling comfortable boarding his dog with us. For the first time in a long while, wife, husband, and dog were all happy.

It's been 12 years since I opened Cold Nose Lodge. Initially, I did worry that I'd lose customers over my policy against the use of prong collars, but I realized that someone who would refuse to use our services for that reason wasn't my ideal client. I also hold myself to the same standards. I would never actively do anything to cause fear in an animal or their owners.

A good life for dogs is the biggest success for me.

▦ **My biggest challenge:** I launched my business during the 2008 financial crisis and recession, so I know how to get through lean times.

A good life for dogs is the biggest success for me.

When the pandemic hit in the spring of 2020, I feared my business might not survive the stay-at-home order and the health crisis that made people afraid to go out.

I could have shut down, but I did my research, came up with a plan, and got a Paycheck Protection Program loan. I'm happy to say the Lodge is going to make it and will emerge better than ever. I had started a renovation project before the pandemic, but thankfully the bulk of the work hadn't been started. Once we're solidly back on our feet, we'll continue moving forward with our expansion.

My training: I wanted to be a subject area expert, so I got a degree to be a veterinary technician and worked at a veterinary practice for four years. I received training at Purdue University on the fundamentals of how dogs learn, and I do continuing education courses with a focus on different topics so my knowledge is well-rounded and current.

My hiring philosophy: I aim for diversity and inclusion. It's extremely important to me that I hire people from a variety of backgrounds, ethnicities, religions, and sexual orientation. I also use volunteers from several local nonprofit organizations that support people with all types of disabilities. We have hired staff from the Carbon Lehigh Intermediate Unit.

How I schedule my day: I have a default weekly schedule in which I block out time for errands and tasks such as payroll. I have a daily schedule on paper (digital doesn't work for my brain) on which I have a list of what needs to be done. When I reach the end of the list, I very satisfyingly rip out the page. If I don't accomplish all the tasks, I can't rip it out until they're completed.

What I read and listen to: I love mystery and suspense novels. My current favorite authors are Ruth Ware and JP Delaney. I've also listened to Ted Talks, but my listening style has changed during the pandemic because I want an escape from reality. I've been enjoying podcasts such as my favorite, NPR's *Wait, Wait, Don't Tell Me* and Paula Poundstone's *Nobody Listens to Paula Poundstone*. They both help me find humor while still addressing our current reality. Hallmark movies are also my go-to because they will always have a happy ending.

As a Career Coach, I'm Fascinated by What Motivates People

Carol-Anne Minski, PhD, MBA, president and founder
of CMA Leadership Consultants and author of
FOCUS! Get What You Want Out of Life

I've always been curious about what happens that leads to individual motivation and a need for achievement. The typical school of thought is that people are motivated by money, but motivation is about much more than money.

When employees are asked what they want from their jobs, their number one answer is appreciation. In addition to a good, safe work environment, workers have a need to be recognized. Without a way to provide recognition, workplaces are missing a vital piece of what motivates their employees.

I've spent some time helping companies achieve just that. As a consultant, I've worked within organizations to learn about the issues they're facing, and I've talked through the problems with them. Often, the organizations needed to motivate employees and help them feel productive and satisfied in their jobs.

My passion and fascination in this area led me to earn a PhD in organizational development and to start my own career coaching and consulting with businesses. I also teach a professional development class and coach MBA students at Lehigh University.

Over the years, my career has evolved from consulting work to now spending more time working one-on-one with clients to help them with work focus, goal setting, and moving forward in their career and in life.

Believe it or not, we're all self-directed. Our motivation sparks from our desires, rather than from what somebody else wants us to do. Sometimes people don't know what they desire, and in that case, they need to ask themselves questions to understand what they want.

Once my clients understand their desires, we work on goal setting. I teach them to consider their "next right move": looking for the next opportunity that will allow them to make money while pursuing a passion.

In my own career, there have been times when I realized a job wasn't right for me, so I considered my next right move. I wouldn't quit and then look for new employment. I'd make a plan and bide my time until I found the right opportunity. Using this process, I was able to move on to another opportunity within a year.

Another important skill I work on with clients is the job search. The old way of looking for a job—which is the wrong way—would be to write to someone out of the blue and ask if there are job openings at their company. The correct way is to use solid networking skills to find opportunities.

Networking is about establishing relationships. One way to do that is by reaching out to people you've worked with, asking them what they're doing, and telling them what you're doing. You might send an email to a previous coworker that says, "I miss our working relationship. I'm currently a student working on my MBA, and I'm looking to work in marketing in the future. Hope you're doing well. Let's stay in touch."

You might also consider what you can do for your networking contacts. Pass on information or articles in their field or connect them with your contacts in similar positions. Using LinkedIn is a good way to stay in touch by commenting on your contacts' work accomplishments. Keep in mind that it takes about seven communications with someone for them to remember who you are and what you're doing.

Once you have a professional relationship, it makes it easier to say, "I'm looking to work at Amazon. Do you know anyone who works there?"

Practicing My Own Program

These strategies are exactly what I used to get my business up and running. I didn't set up a website and expect business to magically come to me. I was logical about how to get clients, using networking, marketing, and planning to make my business work.

- **How I've helped my clients:** My clients have learned how to set and reach achievable goals. I've helped them finish writing book manuscripts and come up with strategies for their businesses. Ultimately, I help people focus on what's important and reach the goals they've set for themselves.

- **The most challenging part of coaching:** Not giving my clients advice. When I worked as a consultant, I was hired to give advice. But as a coach, I'm hired to guide my clients to find their own way of succeeding.

Networking is about establishing relationships. One way to do that is by reaching out to people you've worked with, asking them what they're doing, and telling them what you're doing.

A mentor helped me finally write my book. When I moved to Jim Thorpe, I joined organizations such as the Association for Training and Development and BW Nice (Business Women Networking Involving Charity and Education) to get to know people. I met Annarose Ingara-Milch, who had published her own book. My book had been in my head for 10 years, but I didn't get it down on paper until 2014, just after I finished my dissertation and earned my PhD. Annarose held weekly phone calls with me and guided me step-by-step to finish the book and get it published.

A key tool I recommend to my clients: In addition to my book, I created a focus planning journal, which is a calendar/journal in which you organize your goals into a monthly and weekly schedule to keep yourself on track. I use it myself.

How I set my daily schedule: The first task of the day is to feed my kitten and give her attention. Then I go to my computer and my planning journal to see what I have planned for the day. I do a quick email check and then launch into whatever is the most important task for me to accomplish that day. When I'm teaching a class, I do that in the mornings. Once I've completed that, I take a walk for exercise and then I spend the afternoon making phone calls and holding Zoom calls with clients. I set my schedule this way because I'm more productive and creative in the morning.

What I read and watch: I've been watching Ted Talks lately, mostly related to grief because I lost my husband in March 2020. I also watch Ted Talks related to motivation, resilience, and grit.

As for books, I love mysteries and time travel stories. My favorites include *The Time Traveler's Wife* by Audrey Niffenegger and *Leaving Time* by Jodi Picoult.

As a Therapist, I Know the Power of Music and Art in Health

Kathy Purcell, MT-BC, director of Therapeutic Arts Group,
the parent company of Music Therapy Associates, LLC
and Art Therapy Associates, LLC in Whitehall

I realized at an early age that music has undeniable power over us—power to excite, relax, motive, inspire, soothe, and even heal. Knowing this and having a passion for music inspired me to launch my music therapy business 31 years ago to help people live more successful, engaged, and happy lives.

As a child growing up in rural Maryland, I studied classical guitar and enjoyed performing, but I knew there must be something more to music than practicing for hours and striving to play each piece perfectly. My mother heard about an innovative profession called music therapy. When she told me about it, I drove 40 minutes to the library to learn more. Combining my love of music with my desire to help others by becoming a music therapist became my dream. Because the field of music therapy was so new, my parents encouraged me to also get a degree in music education—in case "that whole therapy thing doesn't work out." I followed their advice and earned two bachelor's degrees with a minor in psychology in four years, graduating magna cum laude from Shenandoah Conservatory of Music in Winchester, Virginia.

Desiring to learn more about how music therapy could benefit people with psychiatric diagnoses, I completed my internship at Allentown State Hospital. To my surprise, I fell in love with a wonderful recreation therapist and amazing musician, and he soon became my husband. Shortly after getting married, I began working as a music teacher at what is now KidsPeace. To fulfill my desire to benefit people through music therapy, my husband and I founded Music Therapy Associates (MTA) in 1990. Our sons, Corey and Connor, were brought into this musical world soon thereafter.

Because music therapy was not widely known, I set up information tables and provided interactive music programs at health fairs and parent support groups to inform the public about the benefits of music therapy. To network with other professionals, I joined Lehigh Valley Aging in Place.

Here at MTA, we help people of all ages and abilities, including those recovering from strokes, injuries, and surgeries, as well as people with diagnoses of autism, Down Syndrome, cerebral palsy, traumatic brain injury, Alzheimer's disease, and dementia, among others. We design individual treatment goals based on a client's interests, needs, and functioning level. We also are included in students' Individual Education Plans (IEPs) through schools as a related service under the Individuals with Disabilities Education Act (IDEA). Additionally, MTA provides services through three of the Pennsylvania State Waiver programs and works with many private insurance companies.

Music can benefit people in so many ways. For our clients who have had a stroke and are experiencing a deficit on one side of the body, music therapy helps them overcome muscle weakness. If they're focusing on shaking a maraca or strumming a guitar, they're not thinking about how difficult it might be to use one side of the body. For clients involved in physical therapy after surgery, we can design a music therapy program with music that motivates them, played at just the right speed to help them complete their exercises successfully and gain strength—while having fun! A family told us that through music therapy, their adult child, who has disabilities that make communication difficult, said, "I love you" for the first time. Music is processed throughout the entire brain and can stimulate areas of the brain that our clients have difficulty with, such as those associated with speech and language and motor skills. We are also able to teach clients non-verbal ways to communicate using music.

In 2012, my son Corey joined MTA as the assistant director. His degrees in business marketing and business management from DeSales University doubled our administrative staff.

In response to an increasing number of inquiries from people seeking art therapy, I founded Art Therapy Associates in 2018. Our therapists often use an interdisciplinary approach to offer clients a wider variety of expressive opportunities.

During MTA's 30th year, we formed a "parent company," Therapeutic Arts Group (TAG). We are looking forward to expanding our services as we consolidate our marketing and administrative functions. Today, TAG has grown to 28 music therapists, two music teachers, and four art therapists. We now provide music and art therapy programs to hundreds of people throughout

Pennsylvania and parts of New Jersey every week. I have been working with the PA Music Therapy State Task Force for years to assist with legislation to create a license for the profession of music therapy in Pennsylvania.

Because art and music are such powerful motivators, they are used by therapists to modify and reinforce goals that are not necessarily music or art related. The vast variety of styles and genres of music and art equip therapists with an enormous toolbox for creating sessions designed to engage their clients. Although music therapy and art therapy are not the same as music and art instruction, TAG is also able to provide traditional and adaptive art, instrumental and vocal lessons, and enrichment programs. It is important to know that prospective clients do not need musical skill or artistic talent to benefit from our programs. TAG therapists and teachers work with every-one—from beginner to professional.

- **I strive to be a problem solver:** 2020 brought the worldwide COVID-19 pandemic and unique challenge of providing therapy while wearing a mask. Our facial expressions are very important during therapy, so I developed a special clear plastic face shield with a cloth attachment, which I named ClearProtex. This system provides protection for the wearer as well as those around them. It allows the wearer to breathe and communicate more effectively by allowing the entire face to be visible. We are also providing music and art therapy virtually through online telehealth portals. Since March 2020, we've offered a free daily livestreamed program called Music Made Mobile through our Facebook page.

- **Our logos are a family affair:** Although my husband and I created the original Music Therapy Associates logo, our son Connor, a graphic artist, helped design the Art Therapy Associates logo and the Therapeutic Arts Group logo, which blends together the MTA and the ATA logos to depict music and art combining to provide engagement with love.

- **We look forward to future growth:** The growth and success of both businesses and the formation of Therapeutic Arts Group has led us to commit to opening a permanent site where, in addition to providing services for clients in their homes, day programs, and other community locations, in-person services will be provided in a specifically designed environment. In 2019, I found the perfect building in Whitehall to house Therapeutic Arts Group, which I fondly refer to as the "TAG Building." Through the help and support of family, therapists, teachers, and staff, I am excited to work with the whole TAG family to enrich the lives of many more people through music and art—hopefully for another 31 years!

It's not about Hockey; It's What Hockey Is about— and How That Guided Me in Business

Mike Lichtenberger, Certified Payments Professional, Fellow of the Institute for Independent Business, and founder and group executive of enTrust Merchant Services, a company of Sherwood Management Group LLC, in Bethlehem.

Ice hockey has always been more than just an avocation. Originally from Buffalo, I was fortunate to have played youth hockey then Juniors and briefly in college. To this day, I am totally immersed in the game, but now through coaching. A highlight was coaching my son for many years in youth and scholastic hockey. For over a decade I was the head ice hockey coach for Lehigh University and since 1999 I am a coach developer and Coach-in-Chief for USA Hockey. I believe it is because of my lifelong involvement in the game that I found success in my executive career and later as a business owner. The game certainly gave me a perspective for organizational leadership, staff development, and customer relations. While coaching, I adopted a "players first" philosophy and of course that has now morphed into a "customer first" mindset. We call it Merchant Care. It is about doing what is best for others.

I believe ice hockey always gave me a leg up in problem solving, teamwork, and harmony, and the wonderful connections I made. My ice hockey experience was often the reason I was recruited, and it was certainly a focal point in interviews. These connections gave me early traction in the first few years of owning my own business. The business landscape looks a lot like the game itself. When playing or coaching the game—or running a business—it is our job to solve a series of small problems. It's all about competition, hard work, resilience, and knowing it's okay to fail—even if you fail hard. In business or sport, you succeed or you learn! Of course, winning solves a lot of problems!

Learning never ends, and education is never wasted. I proved this over a 25-year career in corporate risk and regulatory affairs. I worked for large companies: BOC Gases, United Technologies/Carrier, and General Electric. I had become known for mitigating operational risk and major incidents—again, a series of small problems to solve. Despite best practices and receiving many industry awards, compliance became more complex. The markets changed, the boardroom changed, and the playing field changed. So, in 2004, I launched a business advisory company, Sherwood Management Group, named after my father. I counseled clients on operational best practices, quality assurance, regulatory affairs, and insurance risk. In 2007, I acquired a payment processing business and added field sales to my resume.

Whoa! Wait! Sales? It was like being traded, and I had to start over to develop key relationships and a new path. A one-time boss suggested that I would be good in the sales game, and he turned out to be correct.

Branded now as enTrust Merchant Services and organized under Sherwood Management Group, we have a balanced portfolio. Longevity with account retention is our greatest testimonial for Merchant Care. Business networking was foreign to me, but I quickly learned that spending time with others would result in establishing a presence in the Lehigh Valley.

I chair the Business Council of the Lehigh Valley Chamber and serve on the Board of Governors. The benefit is seeing that others are willing to share best practices and mentoring. Similar to sports coaching among those we admire, we tend to create an identity and adopt a mindset that "If I do what they do, I will have what they have." I am here to tell you, whether in sports or in business, it takes a lot more than mirroring their practices and styles.

And that's where a lifetime in hockey comes into play. Because I operate independently, I had to write a new sales playbook based on prior skills. The challenges found in running a new business looked a lot like the game of ice hockey. I see exactly where ice hockey and business intersect.

What makes a business owner different from others in a crowded market? What are the traits of a coach whose team wins championships? What may differentiate such a leader? Sport teaches you the necessary life skills, and life skills give you experiences, and experiences give you the patience, perseverance, and resilience to grow.

My competencies show I care about our clients and their success, that I am committed to making a difference, and that trust has to be earned every day. This is Merchant Care, and it is our distinction.

In business or sport, you succeed or you learn!
Of course, winning solves a lot of problems!

Working through the pandemic: Due to mandated closures, I experienced a drop in revenue and net income. I pivoted to a transactional risk model by helping clients navigate disputes and protect sales revenue. Often it was unpaid consulting, but it was more important to me to help others and practice servant leadership. I am happy that I had those opportunities for growth.

Benefits to running a business: Opening my own business helped me take more control of my time and my ambitions. Having control does not mean you get to blame others. But for a breakthrough experience with extraordinary results, we make a shift with a growth mindset toward adopting a positive belief system by turning "I have to..." into "I want to..."

Being involved in the community inspires me in my business. It is important to me that others see the full potential of what is possible, so I set aside time to fundraise and advocate for causes, serve on advisory boards, such as The Chamber and Lehigh Carbon Community College, other appointments like LANta, and, of course, USA Hockey's Coach Development.

What I read and listen to: I enjoy historical biographies of US and European Leaders (Lincoln, Roosevelt, Churchill) and business and sports leadership titles published by the Fellowship of Christian Athletes. My play-list includes The Beatles catalog, The Eagles, Phil Collins, Supertramp, Billy Joel, Boz Scaggs, Elton John, Fleetwood Mac, and James Taylor.

My Approach to Financial Planning: We Are Investment Behavioral Coaches

Mary Evans, CFP, CDFA, a certified financial planner professional, Raymond James registered principal, and owner of Evans Wealth Strategies, in Emmaus

I was successful early in my career. A controller by the time I was 30, I later worked my way to become a vice president at Rodale. But when I was 50, I decided to venture on a new career path, which led to the launch of my own financial planning firm.

I take a different approach than most in this industry because I think as much about my clients' emotional health as I do about financial plans and investments. People don't make decisions solely based on facts. They make them based on their emotions. In my practice, we meet people where they are, and we don't use jargon, pressure, or guilt.

Approaching financial planning this way launched me to new levels of success. I grew my business to become one of the largest firms in Raymond James. My business grew from referrals, and very little advertising. This year, we earned Forbes rankings for best in state and top women wealth advisors. Most importantly, my clients tell me that I've changed their lives. More than ever before, I feel like I'm making a difference.

How I Got Here

Growing up, my family was financially poor, but there was an abundance of love, laughter, and encouragement at home. I was the youngest of five, and my parents wanted me to go to college for home economics. I might have been the only home ec major to sign up for calculus, chemistry, and physics. I didn't finish the program because it clearly wasn't for me.

I took a job as a secretary at a bank, and when my manager realized I couldn't type—but I was quick with math—she asked if I wanted to be an

auditor. It paid more, so I said yes. The bank then paid for my college tuition to get an accounting degree from Temple University.

From there, I entered the Fortune 500 world. I was lucky to have great bosses and mentors. My mother told me that I could learn something from everyone, and she was correct.

I told myself at a young age that I never wanted to worry about finances the way my parents did. I changed jobs several times in the first 20 years of my career, always seeking a higher-level position. I worked to get promotions until there were no more opportunities, and then I'd find a new company where there were additional opportunities.

In many of my jobs, I was the only female executive. I learned how to excel in a male-dominated workplace. During meetings, when a male co-worker cursed, everyone looked at me and apologized. I learned to wear the right suits, and how to curse like a drunken sailor. Even today when I attend events for financial service professionals, people I've just met will turn to my husband—who is not a financial planner—and ask how long he's been in the industry.

Taking a New Road

My jobs have always centered around handling finances for businesses, but I have also always cared about people. With my own company, I could meld the world of finance with the emotional health of my clients. Money is a top stressor, and part of my job is to acknowledge that my clients are worried. We talk about their goals and what's important to them, rather than hashing over charts and graphs. I focus on the outcome, not necessarily the process.

When the market moves up and down, it can be difficult for clients. I get on the phone or Zoom with them, explain what's normal for the market, and explain how we've planned for these moves. In the fall of 2019, my staff and I began setting our clients' portfolios up to weather a recession that we thought would be coming. Were we expecting a worldwide pandemic in 2020? Not a chance, but we were prepared for the market moves when they came.

Also, I've always had everything at the office backed up off-site. So, if the building goes down, or if my staff can't get into work, we could get up and running from home. We mostly did that through snowstorms in the past, but now we're doing it during a pandemic. Foresight pays off, especially when the unexpected happens.

■ **My ambitions:** When I was younger, I wouldn't have said that I was ambitious, but I did have the goal to be an international controller by the

My jobs have always centered around handling finances for businesses, but I have also always cared about people. With my own company, I could meld the world of finance with the emotional health of my clients. Money is a top stressor, and part of my job is to acknowledge that my clients are worried.

age of 30. When I achieved my goal, I was the only female controller at the company out of 100.

- **How acts of kindness from mentors helped propel my career:** I had the best bosses and mentors. They taught me how to really do my job well, how to supervise people, and how to get a promotion. They gave me one opportunity after another.

- **How I plan my day:** I'm often reminded of the expression, "If you want to make God laugh, tell him your plans." I'm an early riser. I get up at 5 am, exercise, set a game plan and priorities, and then other stuff happens.

- **What I read:** About once a year, I reread *The Power of Now: A Guide to Spiritual Enlightenment* by Eckhart Tolle, *The Power of Story: Change Your Story, Change Your Destiny in Business and in Life* by Jim Loehr, and *Man's Search for Meaning* by Viktor E. Frankl.

  Other recent reads include *Educated: A Memoir* by Tara Westover, *Origins: How Earth's History Shaped Human History* by Lewis Dartnell, *The Great Influenza: The Story of the Deadliest Pandemic in History* by John M. Barry, *The Panic of 1907: Lessons Learned from the Market's Perfect Storm* by Robert F. Bruner and Sean D. Carr, and *How Not to Diet: The Groundbreaking Science of Healthy, Permanent Weight Loss* by Michael Greger, MD, FACLM.

Good Sleep Is a Lifelong Gift My Company Brings to Families

Ronee Welch, owner and CEO of Sleeptastic Solutions and regional director and board member of the Association of Professional Sleep Consultants

My own struggle to get my twin daughters to sleep through the night when they were infants sparked the idea for my business.

They were six months old at the time, and although their pediatrician said they were old enough to sleep through the night without needing a feeding, they were still getting up at 4 am like clockwork. I had an older daughter who didn't have trouble sleeping through the night, so this was new territory for me.

I bought a book about getting your baby to sleep, and I followed the program. Lo and behold, within a few weeks, my girls were sleeping soundly without waking. Even better, we had a schedule throughout the day and night that worked well for my family. Later, when my son was born, I wasted no time going back to the program and using it to get him on a sleep schedule. It was a success again.

I was a stay-at-home mom during this time, but by the time my son was three, I was ready to try to straddle both worlds. I wanted to have one foot in the business world and one foot at home, taking care of my family. And I decided that if I was going to sell something, it had to be a product or service I really believed in.

Because the sleep program worked so well for us and because I knew getting enough sleep was a huge issue for new families, I got certified in the sleep program I used with my kids. Over the years, I stopped being affiliated with that particular program and created my own program that I believe works best, given my expertise in multiple areas.

One of the most important lessons I teach my clients is that your baby already has a schedule, whether or not you've recognized it. When you learn their schedule, it's important to first meet them where they are and then work on getting them onto a schedule that works best for the family, if possible. Sometimes families want their kids to adhere to a sleep schedule that's just not realistic, but they can improve their child's sleep schedule while honoring the routine their child naturally gravitates toward.

My identical twins are a perfect example. You'd think their sleep needs would be identical, but their schedule was about a half hour off from each other. As they've gotten older, their sleep needs have continued to fluctuate. The twin who gave me a hard time as an infant is the one who sleeps the best today. The other twin has stayed on a more regimented, consistent schedule.

Once your family is sleeping well, everything else will fall into place. You can manage your daytime so much better when your baby has good naps, fewer meltdowns, an improved mood, and is more open to playing and learning. Some of the families I've worked with have said that I saved their marriage and helped them feel less angry, frustrated, and anxious every day.

■ **Expanding my expertise:** When I first started Sleeptastic Solutions, I never envisioned where my journey would take me. I wanted to be an expert in all of the issues that affect the way people sleep. I'm a sleep consultant, first and foremost, and my business will always be centered around sleep, but I've added new services that have become branches to my tree.

In addition to being certified as a pediatric sleep consultant, I'm also a certified:

- Holistic and integrative adult sleep coach, utilizing a combination of life changes and cognitive behavioral therapy for insomniacs (CBT-I).
- Postpartum doula (CPD)
- Lactation counselor (CLC)
- Infant massage educator (CEIM)
- Parenting coach, using a love and boundaries approach for children of any age
- Holistic nutrition coach, specializing in prenatal, postnatal, and family nutrition
- Holistic health and lifestyle coach

All of my certifications and areas of expertise combine to give me a true understanding of why a child, teen, or adult isn't sleeping well and what needs to be done to fix the problem. My expertise in all of these areas sets me apart from my competitors. I also have a tremendous amount of drive and passion for helping families.

A few years ago, I added online courses to the mix, which has helped my business thrive as our lives moved online during the pandemic.

Good sleep is a gift that lasts a lifetime. The sleep habits children learn when they're young will help them when they're teenagers and adults. The adults I work with who have insomnia often had sleep problems during childhood that were never fixed.

Marketing and collaborations: I do a lot of networking and collaborations online, particularly through Facebook groups. This led to an agency in a nearby county hiring me to work with 15 teen moms as a postpartum doula. I created a private online course and hold virtual calls with the moms where I teach them parenting and life skills, as well as answering their questions. It's some of the most rewarding work I've done!

When another business owner wants to collaborate, I never say no, even if it means doing something for free, because word of mouth goes a long way in getting more business. I recently provided my services through a virtual Zoom call to refugee women in Texas for free, and it was very fulfilling!

How I schedule my day: I'm a fanatic about scheduling. Typically, I work a regular workday while my kids are in school. When they're home for the summer, I plan my schedule around fun activities.

Having to quarantine during the pandemic certainly threw things off this year, but I am doing my best to adjust my schedule to work while my kids are in "school" (aka on Zoom calls in a nearby room). I'm able to continue to work with my Sleeptastic clients while studying to become a Board Certified Lactation Consultant (IBCLC) both during the day and at night after my kids go to bed.

What I read: Right now, all of my reading is related to my certification courses, any research I'm following up on for my clients, and to stay current in my respective fields.

In a Socially Distanced World, Audiovisual Collaboration Helps Keep Us Connected

Jeffrey French, CTS-D, founder of French Curve LLC, provides audiovisual design and build services including customized audiovisual workstations.

French Curve LLC audiovisual design is a truly unique company in the Lehigh Valley. We are a local provider of audiovisual design services. Our services are focused on the communication and workflow of the client. We believe a wholistic design approach will extend the best value to owners and stakeholders in the long term.

Imagine teaching an online class, giving a slideshow presentation to a group of colleagues, or speaking to a group from a lectern—and having it all go smoothly without technical issues. That's one of my goals as an audiovisual designer. No one wants to present in front of a group of people—live or virtually—and have the technology fail. It's not only frustrating and stressful, but an inefficient loss of time. When you have an AV system specifically in alignment with your workflow, the technology is predictable and provides for a confident user experience.

I set out to create a uniquely designed system specifically for my clients. While I cannot guarantee clients will never experience a glitch, I strive to eliminate potential problems. I look for that "aha!" moment when my clients realize their workflow is improved and the audiovisual system enables them to communicate effectively. That is a successful day in my business.

Getting past the "pain point": One of the real pleasures of my business is helping people become comfortable with using technology. The complexity of technology often leads people to a "pain point," when a component of the system fails and results in a frustrating or embarrassing moment in front of a group of people. The fear of that occurrence can make clients reluctant to use

the technology. When I can design a system and improve my client's workflow and minimize those pain points, I know I've done my job.

Audiovisual system design begins with listening to the client's needs and creating a comprehensive plan. I have a good understanding of the audiovisual manufacturers and their respective product lines. Based on this knowledge, I can integrate the most appropriate equipment with the system. As a consultant, I am not influenced by product sales volumes or agreements, so I can implement the absolute best combination of products that are in the best interest of my clients.

What sets me apart from AV systems design in the Lehigh Valley? I work with my clients in the early stages of planning. One benefit of starting with the conception of a project is I can review and modify infrastructure related items, such as wiring paths and equipment locations, to minimize points of conflict later. I can also select equipment that meets the aesthetics intended by the architect.

Design work includes project management throughout the project execution to insure proper installation of the system. While it can vary by each project, I engage with the stakeholders including owners, architects, engineers, interior designers, consultants, and contractors.

With an understanding of the foundational principles, a good design can transform offices, conference rooms, churches, classrooms, gymnasiums, and stadiums into communication centers—complete with clear audio and sharp video.

The pandemic has challenged the audiovisual industry at a historic level. The role technology plays in communication and collaboration is more demanding than ever before. We have turned to digital conferencing tools to comply with safety and social distancing guidelines, and this has created a global surge in demand for remote workforce solutions.

In response to the need for these remote work systems, French Curve has designed customizable workstations that include network access and collaboration and screen sharing tools. Designed for personal use, they are appropriate for educators, students, and professionals working from any location including home offices, classrooms, and offices. The primary focus of the workstations is ergonomic comfort, aesthetics, and efficiency.

▦ **My advice to entrepreneurs:** I launched French Curve in August of 2019. The most difficult part of the process of getting up and operating was making the decision to start my own business. Once I had conferred with my mentors and made up my mind this was the direction to follow,

The most difficult part of the process of getting up and running was making the decision to start my own business in the first place. Once I had conferred with my mentors and made up my mind that I wanted to do this, the mechanics of setting up the business were pretty easy.

the mechanics of setting up the business were easy. Registering a limited liability company (LLC) through the PA One Stop Shop has been simplified, making it much easier than I had expected.

Resources such as the Small Business Development Centers, state-funded centers, and the nonprofit SCORE are important partners in your journey. They connect you with subject matter experts, instructional webinars, and other resources. All are invaluable in guiding you through the process.

How I schedule my day: It's simple, but it works. I use Microsoft, OneNote for my action items list. It is a digital version of a to-do list with little boxes to check off once I have completed the tasks. My action list, which I prioritize daily, stays open all day on one of my computer screens, so I have a visual reminder of my priorities for each day.

What I read and watch: I enjoy reading action and adventure fiction including James Paterson, David Badacci and Ken Follett. I also enjoy new perspectives on history such as Chris Wallace's *Countdown 1945: The Extraordinary Story of the Atomic Bomb and the 116 Days That Changed the World*. I am also an outdoor enthusiast with hiking and mountain biking high on the favorites list. As a member of Valley Mountain Bikers, I work with a group of volunteers who build and maintain trails at the Trexler Nature Preserve in Schnecksville, PA.

I keep up with technology trends by following key contributors in digital media and attending product and technology webinars by manufacturers and industry associations. It's extremely helpful in keeping current within the audiovisual industry.

I'm Always Prepared for Swings in the Title Industry

Victor A. Cimerol, co-owner of and director of sales for First United Land Transfer, in Allentown and Bethlehem

My father always told me that I would be a business owner, and that was perfectly fine with me. With my brother, Bob, as my business partner, we've owned half a dozen companies since 1980, including a printing company, a restaurant, a home builder business, and a trucking company. In 2006, we started First United Land Transfer, a title insurance agency that's still going strong today.

We achieved different levels of success with each company, but with First United Land Transfer, we're seeing the success we always hoped to achieve. There are a few things that got us to where we are today: We keep the business local and do it the best we can; we give our clients a good experience; and we prepare for the swings that inevitably occur in the title insurance industry.

Title insurance protects real estate owners and lenders against losses that might occur if there's a question about the property's ownership, such as a prior lien or a missing heir. As part of our services, we conduct a search of public records to show the current and past ownership of the property going back at least 60 years, making sure all the deed transfers were done correctly. When issues arise, sometimes they can be cleared and removed from the public record. There are times when title issues can't be cleared. Some, we can resolve with an indemnity from the last title policy. Others, the only way to clear the issue is with a legal process. Once the deal closes, we record the new deed and mortgage into the public record.

The two title policies are an owner policy and a loan policy. The owner policy protects the owner. The loan policy protects the lender's mortgage. Most of our referrals come from lenders and Realtors who complete a lot of real estate transactions, and they keep coming back to us because of the customer service we offer and the assurance we provide. But we've also seen a trend in consumers becoming more educated about title insurance and calling our office to learn more about what we offer. I enjoy answering questions and helping consumers make informed choices.

I didn't have experience in title insurance when we started First United Land Transfer, but Bob had worked for another title agency in Philadelphia. He had the idea of using his experience at the title agency as a springboard to start our own business in the Lehigh Valley.

Our first goal was to keep the business local and to develop strong relationships with our clients. National title agencies cover large areas, but we decided to stick with our backyard of Pennsylvania and New Jersey and to do our job well.

We also focus on the experience we give our clients. Most real estate brokers own a title insurance agency and bring their buyers to their agency. The only way to compete is to give our clients a good experience that keeps them coming back to us and encourages them to recommend us to others in the industry.

There's one more very important aspect to our success. We've learned to anticipate and prepare for swings in our industry. During our first seven years in the market, refinance transactions made up most of our business, thanks to lower interest rates. But after 2013, interest rates went up, and refinances pretty much ended. We shifted our focus to include purchase transactions and our relationships with Realtors. We learned that focusing on just one aspect of the business wasn't a good strategy for survival when the economy changes, so we diversified.

Surviving Challenges

Having that foresight has helped us through the pandemic. Before 2020, in Pennsylvania there was no legislation that allowed a notary to do remote online notarization. However, we knew the legislation would be coming and wanted to be prepared. Three years ago, we signed up with a company that allowed us to do remote online notarization so we would be ready. Then the pandemic hit, and much of the business in the Lehigh Valley was shut down in March 2020, but the government enabled remote online notarization.

We were one of the few companies set up to do closings online, and we were able to stay in business during the shutdown. We didn't advertise our ability to conduct remote online closings because we didn't want to benefit from other companies' misfortunes, but we completed the transactions we had in the pipeline and ended up increasing our revenue over the course of the year. Some of our competitors even reached out and asked how we did it, and we talked them through getting set up.

There's one more very important aspect to our success. We've learned to anticipate and prepare for swings in our industry.

We went from having a very robust amount of business to doing twice that amount, but we always have an eye toward what might happen in the future, and we try to prepare for that swing. The next year might present another challenge, but we'll meet the challenge by fulfilling the expectations of our clients.

- **Persistence paid off:** I attribute having a successful business to the continuity of "keep trying." I could have chosen not to take my dad's advice about becoming a business owner. Working for a large company would have allowed a comfortable living, but I'm glad I went down the road I did. My dad was a home builder, owned a flower shop, and then owned real estate and imposed his wisdom on me.

- **How I structure my day:** Everyone in the office sees my calendar. My brother is involved with managing our employees and the title-clearing decisions, making sure the daily operations are completed. I intentionally don't get involved with that side of the business. I trust his judgment and do more of the face-to-face meetings and building relationships with our clients. I spend my day talking to Realtors and lenders and conducting settlements.

- **What I listen to:** That's always evolving. I listen to the news and podcasts, including language podcasts.

Success Has a Deeper Meaning Now That I Bring Relief to Families in Crisis

Pam Bartlett, owner of Senior Helpers of the Lehigh Valley

I am in the "Peace of Mind" business.

After a 30+ year career working for nationally branded consumer products companies, retailers were consolidating, and jobs in marketing and sales were disappearing. In 2013, my employer left the area, and I knew there was not much of a future for the industry in the Lehigh Valley.

I had to make a choice about what to do next, and the idea of buying a franchise appealed to me. It is a business that comes with a recipe, and I knew I could add my own spice as an entrepreneur. I hired a franchise consultant, who suggested a handful of different types of businesses I could pursue. I had known for years I was missing something in my previous employment.

One of the ideas the franchise consultant presented was senior care, and it spoke to me. I had lost my parents in 2008 and 2009 and spent two years taking care of my in-laws, who both had Alzheimer's disease. I had a deep understanding of how difficult it can be when family members go from being independent to dependent and quality time turns into caregiving. Suddenly, I realized my degree in rehabilitation services fit perfectly into my new opportunity.

My next step was to explore different senior care franchises. I narrowed my search, and I did a lot of research, made a lot of calls, and asked a lot of questions. The deciding factor was that Senior Helpers had a commitment to senior care and a strong franchisee support system. I bought the business in 2013, and I know that I made a great decision with this brand. Education and support are necessary to be successful in this industry. There is a lot at stake, and people's lives are in our hands.

Success for me today is about changing people's lives.

We offer a range of services, from companionship, running errands, or

light housekeeping, to in-depth specialized care. We also care for seniors who are at the end of life and receiving hospice care, seniors with Alzheimer's disease, dementia, Parkinson's disease, or other chronic illnesses. We have a specialized, proprietary dementia training program provided to our care specialists on their first day.

In some cases, we work with a client throughout every stage. For example, we started caring for one of our seniors about five years ago. She was experiencing depression and anxiety. Our care specialist went to her house two or three days a week to spend time with her and take her shopping. They played Scrabble, making sure our client won because that was important to her. It helped her feel less lonely.

Over the years, she needed more services. Today, she is 99 years old and on hospice. She is bedbound, so our care specialists give her bed baths, move her in the bed to avoid bedsores, conduct incontinence care, cook for her, clean her home, and keep her company. They make sure she has everything she needs. She's receiving care from us 24 hours a day, seven days a week.

Families tend to call us when they are in crisis mode; an aging parent needs help, and the family cannot do it alone anymore. Many of them are members of the sandwich generation now managing the lives of parents and young children. Most families are not aware of the resources that are available, so we work with them to coordinate services and ensure their loved ones' needs are met.

We offer relief. When a family calls looking for help, we conduct a complimentary in-home care assessment. Our care manager, who is a Certified Senior Advisor, meets with the client and family and completes a detailed assessment of the senior's health, home, safety issues, nutrition, support, and other aspects of the senior's physical and mental health. From there, the plan of care is created.

Our goal is to help people age safely wherever they call home. We also give adult children the opportunity to spend quality time with their aging parents. Some of the care we provide is for people who are in assisted living situations, but most of it is in the home. In some cases, long-term care insurance and veterans' benefits cover our services.

We believe in giving back to the community we serve. For example, we have provided free dementia training. We have trained first responders who are often called to seniors' homes in crisis situations, and we brought nationally renowned dementia expert Teepa Snow to the Lehigh Valley for a day of dementia education, which was attended by about 300 people. We held a session for clinicians and a session for families. I also serve on the board of directors of our local senior center.

One may be familiar with the term, "It takes a village." This is true with senior care. I could not do this on my own, and I am fortunate to have a wonderful, dedicated team both behind the scenes and in our seniors' homes. Most of our team will say it is not just a job, but a calling, and it is apparent in the care and dedication of our office staff and care specialists. We provide free ongoing training to keep our care specialist on the cutting edge of best practices for our seniors.

Families say we are life savers because we are available 24/7, and we bring care and concern to our jobs. When I say, "We're in the Peace of Mind Business," it is the peace of mind that we provide to families.

- **My biggest challenge:** I have watched my business grow and thrive over the past few years. However, we are in a difficult period because there is a shortage of caregivers nationally and in the Lehigh Valley. At the same time, there is a huge demand for caregiving services, especially as families try to avoid putting loved ones in group facilities because of the pandemic. It's harder to grow because we don't have enough help. In some cases, we have had to turn away business.

- **How I set my daily schedule:** I am currently working from home because of COVID-19, but I get up at the same time every day and come downstairs showered and dressed as if I am going to the office. I stick to the structure of the traditional workday, even though I am running a 24/7 business. We have an answering service and after-hours schedulers who are on the clock when the office is closed. The downside of running this business is that it can be stressful, and I forget to take breaks. I constantly check my phone and email even when I am on vacation because, even though I am away from it, I never stop caring about the people for whom we are responsible. My team and I are dedicated to make sure all calls and issues are addressed.

- **What I read:** It is a priority that I keep up with industry information, current events, and proposed legislation. I am reading daily updates and learning about new modalities and concepts in home care. I am also an avid reader of fiction and read an average of four to five books a month. It's my escape from stress. I keep a book journal where I write the date I finish each book, a rating of how much I liked it, and some notes.

Our Customers Get One-of-a-Kind Expertise in the Lehigh Valley

Chris Schmidt, vice president of operations at the
Keystone Running Store, in Allentown

Sometimes people walk into our store and see a shoe on the shelf and ask to try it on, and then we have to tell them that's not how we do things. In order to give our customers the very best-fitting shoes, we take the time to measure their feet, look at their foot shape, look at the wear on an old pair of shoes, watch them walk or run, and talk to them about who they are and what they do.

Once we've taken those steps, we give them three or four pairs of shoes to try on and watch them walk and run in them before making a recommendation about which shoe we think is best.

Runners make up at least half of our customers. The experience and expertise we bring to our customers means their athletic shoes give them the proper support for the miles they put in.

The other half of our customers includes walkers, people who are on their feet all day, and people who've been sent to us by doctors or physical therapists because they're experiencing foot pain or another issue. Simply getting the right shoe for the size and shape of their foot sometimes relieves their pain. If they need orthotic inserts, we also offer them.

We've had customers say we gave them the best shopping experience of their lives. No other shoe store in the Lehigh Valley does what we do. I personally train every staff member on how to take care of people's feet and how to teach our customers to take care of their feet.

My experience fitting people for shoes began 30 years ago when I worked for Hush Puppies at the mall. My boss taught me how to take measurements and how to talk to people about what they needed. I moved on to work for a sporting goods store and was the only employee who took the time to listen to and fit my customers.

I was interested in learning more, so I went to school to become a pedorthist and became certified to make and repair shoes and orthotics, although I didn't continue the certification because I didn't want to spend my nights repairing shoes. However, it gave me a foundation about the biomechanics of people's feet and an understanding of what people need from footwear.

I have a keen interest in taking care of people, and I see things a little differently than most people. When I look at someone walk, I can tell if they're out of alignment. At a glance, I can tell if someone is wearing the wrong size shoe.

The Keystone Running Store opened in February 2020 in Allentown, but it had previously been The Finish Line Running Store, which was opened in 1981 by Jim Stewart. I started working for Jim in 1987 and decided to buy the business in 1997. At the time, I saw that running as a sport was growing, and I noticed more women were coming into the store. I started making a shift to stock more women's shoes and apparel and focus our advertising on women, and the business took off.

The Finish Line moved to Emmaus in 2007 and closed in 2013. Today, I'm vice president of operations for the Keystone Running store and bring my years of experience and expertise to the job.

- **What brought me success:** I became successful by being a real person. I'm up-front and honest with people. I'd rather send someone out of the store with nothing than with a pair of shoes that's not right for them. The first and most important thing is customer service, because nothing else happens if you don't have customers. If my staff and I do the best job we can every day, everything falls into place, and people leave the store as friends.

- **How we dealt with the challenge of 2020:** We opened the store just before the pandemic hit and stores were forced to close—but that didn't stop us from fitting our customers. I relied strongly on social

The first and most important thing is customer service, because nothing else happens if you don't have customers.

I became successful by being a real person. I'm up-front and honest with people. I'd rather send someone out of the store with nothing than with a pair of shoes that's not right for them.

media and word of mouth among our customers. We started doing virtual fittings in which customers send videos of their feet and measure their feet with a ruler. They've been a success. In every case, we paired people with the right shoes for their feet.

The most common problem we see: Many of our customers who come in complaining of foot pain are wearing shoes that are too small. They think that if they paid upwards of $200 for them, they must be good shoes, but what they really need is a good evaluation and fitting.

In one case, a customer came in whose doctor had told him he needed an orthotic insert and possibly surgery. He had lost weight and had been walking for exercise, but his feet were killing him. I looked at what he was wearing and knew right away his shoes were the wrong size and that he needed more support. We took the measurements, watched him walk in our shoes, and found a pair to recommend. He said they felt great. Realizing they're in the wrong size is the first "aha!" moment our customers tend to have.

Community connection has always been part of my business: When I owned The Finish Line, I stayed connected with the Lehigh Valley Road Runners and First Strides, a women's running group. I use running to keep my weight down and to relieve stress, and I ran a couple of marathons in the past for the Leukemia & Lymphoma Society, raising money for a child with leukemia.

I also have a long relationship with podiatrists, orthopedic surgeons, and physical therapists in the Lehigh Valley. I've been hosting doctor nights since I was working for Jim at The Finish Line. I'd let them know what we did at the store, and the word would spread so that customers would come to us on the advice of their doctors.

Success Comes from Helping Others Be Successful

Laurie A. Siebert, CPA, CFP, AEP, senior vice-president
of Valley National Financial Advisors and host of the WDIY radio show
Your Financial Choices with Laurie A. Siebert

I wanted to be a teacher. Once I enrolled in college, there were limited teaching jobs in my home state of Michigan. I quit in my sophomore year, but I was encouraged to return. Nine months later, I was at a new school as an accounting major, working to pay my way. I went from being a drugstore sales clerk to a store manager. I was 22 and female, among 26 male store managers. I went on to get an accounting job at a local CPA firm where the owner told me that maybe accounting was not for me. While I loved the problem-solving, I struggled with the limited exposure to people. I had loved the people side of retail. I went on to have a few other accounting jobs, but I still did not find what I needed.

Eventually, I landed at a law firm, Noonan Law Office, where I did mostly estate and trust tax work. This job changed everything for me. From attorney Charlie Noonan, I learned the value of knowing your clients, being empathetic, and taking the time to help them understand complex issues while navigating their emotional needs at a very vulnerable time. Leaving there after nine years was one of the hardest decisions of my life because I could not see what I was going toward, but I knew there was something else I needed.

That something else led me to Valley National Financial Advisors in January 2000. I started part-time as a CPA and within several months obtained my broker's license and my CFP professional designation. Soon, I was helping with the start-up of a trust company and doing financial planning for clients. Tom Riddle, owner of Valley National Financial Advisors, had confidence in me and foresight to give me an opportunity when I asked, "Why can't we work with all of our clients like this?" Within a few years, I was running one of our wealth management businesses. We navigated a move away from strictly the buying and selling of investments to a more client-needs focus along with coordinated planning. This was long before it became the trend. We launched a new, customer relationship management system, portfolio reporting and rebalancing system, and planning

software that integrated everything. At the time, only a small group of top advisors in the country were using this method, and it provided efficiencies to allow continued growth.

Several years ago, I stepped away from business management and back to a client-focused engagement. While I have often been encouraged to start my own business, I've made a conscious decision to spend my time focusing on what I love doing, which is helping and educating people, not running a business. If I am professionally successful in my career because of helping others to be personally successful, I am fulfilled. If you take care of your clients, your business will be successful. In addition, I have had the opportunity to host a live financial education radio show called *Your Financial Choices with Laurie A. Siebert* on WDIY 88.1FM, airing in the Lehigh Valley and New Jersey. My most important words at the end of every show are "be proactive, not reactive." I find it very applicable in our business. Make the most informed decisions and be happy with those choices with no regrets.

Some of us understand what success means for ourselves and achieve it. Some of us happen upon success by accident. And for some, success eludes. Success can come fast, slow, in waves, or what might feel like never. I am a believer in visualization. Visualize success for you. Success does not happen without hard work. My parents had a strong work ethic. My mother, Cecilia Root, taught us to be confident in our abilities, to be true to ourselves, and to be resourceful. She is the greatest example of compassion, empathy, love, hard work, confidence, tenacity, and resourcefulness that I have ever had.

■ **Success does not happen without a team.** My husband married me despite knowing that I have workaholic tendencies and loves me just the way I am. It takes a village, and my husband is one all by himself. His endless support of me has opened the door for me to explore many opportunities. My children and son-in-law appreciate that I love what I do, and I want to be their role model. My siblings and in-laws teach me about empathy, kinship, family dynamics, and real-world situations that families face.

I have learned that success is experienced every day by making a difference for someone else and believing in your own worth.

I am a believer in visualization.

Visualize success for you.

Over the years, I have seen the strength of women, and I know and understand their power and worth, having witnessed firsthand many women continuing to work while managing the unimaginable. My sister and sister-in-law, Vivian Root and Rosemarie Barbeau, have always helped me figure out the important aspects of my deliberations. My extended family and work colleagues have been role models of hard work and passion in what they do. With this, I have learned that success is experienced every day by making a difference for someone else and believing in your own worth. Have high standards for yourself and those around you and always remain curious.

Nonprofit work: I enjoy being involved in a number of non-profit groups, such as the American Heart Association Circle of Red, which raises awareness for heart and stroke conditions and health. I serve as president of the United Way of the Greater Lehigh Valley Women United affinity group. We are a group of philanthropic women supporting other women and children through education. In the past, I served as president of the Estate Planning Council of the Lehigh Valley. Estate planning is a passion of mine because people struggle to manage this part of their financial life.

Awards: I am proud to be recognized in our community as a Lehigh Valley Business Woman of Influence Circle of Excellence honoree in 2020 and the Women's Business Council of the Greater Lehigh Valley Chamber of Commerce 2017 Athena Leadership Award recipient. Both Lehigh Valley Business and the Women's Business Council contribute so much to our community in delivering news and promoting Lehigh Valley businesses.

What I read:

- *The New York Times* morning and evening briefings
- *The Reporter Who Knew Too Much*, about the reporter Dorothy Kilgallen, by Mark Shaw
- *Outliers: The Story of Success* by Malcolm Gladwell

A Brilliant, Burning Passion for Art and Photography Led Me to Where I Am Today

Terree O'Neill Yeagle, photographer and owner of The Moment Photography in the Lehigh Valley and owner of Wear the Wonder, redefining how you consume art

Life is always changing, and I'm always evolving with it. Starting a photography business in 1993 was a logical step because I've loved taking photos since childhood. Then, I added nature photography to my repertoire and began sharing my work with the world using a unique printing technique.

I've had a camera in my hand since I was eight years old. On school field trips, the other kids had neat little compact cameras, and I always had something that opened and folded out and was larger and cumbersome—but took fantastic pictures.

I launched The Moment Photography after college when I started a family and wanted a career that would allow me to stay home with my kids. I was inspired by a painting of a Native American brave and his wife nestled in each other's arms with their eyes closed, absolutely comforted by each other's presence. The painting is called *The Moment*, which was a revelation for me. I've always thought of photos as little treasures because they capture a moment and a feeling that can be conveyed to the audience. I've photographed thousands of people in beautiful moments ever since.

Life changed again after my kids grew up and moved away. I had spent years taking pictures of them, and now I needed a new subject. I began taking nature photos. I sometimes feel as if I am the camera, and when I see beauty, I must take a picture of it. Sunrises, for instance, happen every day, but every day they're brilliantly different. When I'm driving in the morning while the sun is coming up, I'll have to pull to the side of the road to document it.

A New Business is Born

When I was ready to share my nature photos with the world, I did a few gallery and art shows, but it was costly to create a gallery exhibit. My next inspiration came one day in a museum shop when I found a cuff bracelet with a photo on it.

I did some research and learned that there's a way to print on metal and other materials such as shells. This would be my next evolution: to redefine how we consume art. I invested in the equipment and started putting my photographs on jewelry and items for the home. My photos of winter trees, sunflowers, autumn roses, shells, cardinals, and more are printed on one-of-a-kind cuff bracelets, earrings, necklaces, rings, coasters, and other items, too. I also add haikus to the inside of the bracelets to add something extra special.

In Wear the Wonder, I have a fantastic business partner: my daughter. She joined me a couple of years ago after my husband passed away. She was in town as I was packing up the house and offered to inventory my products and update my website. When she showed me what she had done, I was blown away. I asked her if she wanted to work with me, and she did. I take the photos and design the products here in the Lehigh Valley, and she makes the products in a studio in Cape Cod.

Our intention from the beginning was to sell the items online, and it's going beautifully. We grow a little more each week, and being online allows us to experiment with different designs, creating small batches to test how they sell before we commit to a bigger batch. People buy our products from all over the world.

- **Why I love digital photography:** We all remember film and developing photos in a darkroom. Now photographers download their photos onto a computer and develop their photos in software. I shoot in raw mode and adjust the photos' tones, color balance, brightness, and luminosity. It's a great thing to be able to control so many aspects of an image. I can make a photo look like it does with my eye or with my mind's eye.

- **I speak my dreams out loud:** A while ago, I started noticing that if I spoke about my desires, hopes, and dreams, they would come to pass. When my kids were very young, we lived in a little house in the woods that was busting at the seams with me, my husband, three kids, two dogs, my business, and my husband's business. We had to find a bigger space, and I'd sit in my kitchen and dream of looking out my window and seeing mountains. I began discussing my desire with anybody who would listen, just in casual conversation.

A while ago, I started noticing that if I spoke about my desires, hopes, and dreams, they would come to pass.

We found a piece of land with rolling hills and valleys to build our next home. The many details of the build took my attention, and I stopped thinking about my dream of seeing mountains out my window. We moved in during the summer when the trees were lush with leaves. Several months later during winter, I was drinking tea in my kitchen and glanced out the window. Lo and behold, I saw small mountains—the rolling hills that surrounded the house—peeking through the bare branches.

Over and over in my personal and professional life, I've found that saying things out loud makes them happen, including how I found the location for my first photography studio.

- **My mentors:** My father had a love of photography and got me interested in cameras at a young age, and my mother is a writer and taught me the beauty of words, which helped me document my husband's illness and my journey through grief and loss.

- **How I schedule my day:** I have to see my schedule on paper, so I write myself many notes on Post-its and index cards, but mostly in journals. Using books allows me to doodle and keep track of phone numbers, along with keeping me on schedule. I love storing pieces of my life in books.

- **What I read and listen to:** I collect large, heavy coffee-table books filled with photographs of fashion and art. I also listen to the *Master Class* podcast by Oprah. I enjoy her rambling conversations with guests about things like what influenced them as children and how they got involved in their field.

Real Estate Investing Boosts My Income During Retirement

Robert Sayre, real estate investor and author of *What the 1% Know: How Everyday People Use Real Estate to Build Wealth*

Five years ago, I was reaching retirement, but I wasn't ready to stop learning and growing. I knew some people who had invested in real estate, and that intrigued me. I saw real estate as a way to diversify our investments. It's less liquid than stocks and bonds, but real estate offers better returns, more stability, and the ability to grow in value over time.

The idea of success had changed for me over the years. I had worked as a business manager at the former Emmaus-based publisher Rodale and then helped accounting firms develop marketing plans. Later in my career, I was certified in Six Sigma and worked in process improvement, helping companies create efficiencies in their supply chains and organize their warehouses.

At a certain point, I stopped having career goals, but I still had financial goals. When I decided that I didn't really want to be retired, I knew it was time to move forward with real estate investing.

Going into real estate meant I needed an education in the industry. I'm a lifelong learner, so the idea that I'd have to learn something completely new was a benefit rather than a hindrance to me.

I read books about the industry, went to Meetups with other real estate investors, met a lot of people, and looked at a lot of houses. There's much to learn. Once I had the information and knowledge, I had to have to the confidence to say to my wife, "Let's do this."

My first step was to partner with a friend. We bought two houses in Indiana together, fixed them up, and rented them. That led to looking for local investments, closer to home in the Lehigh Valley, on my own.

I had to keep my goals in mind. Most of the people I met who were real estate investors were about 25 years younger than me and were trying to replace a salary. That's no small thing.

Most wealthy people have real estate as part of their wealth-building strategy. I've seen people put all of their money in real estate for this reason. That's good when the market is doing well, but it puts all your eggs in one basket. Taking that track wasn't going to help me with my goal of diversification.

Reimagining success, for me, was to approach real estate investing in my own way. I wasn't trying to build an empire. I wanted to stick to what was important to me, and that was creating a diversified income with stability and safety.

I received some good advice from a friend: Stick to one thing and do it well. I decided to focus on row homes in the Lehigh Valley and Reading, about 1,200 square feet with three bedrooms and one bathroom. I looked at a lot of houses, and then I bought one in Allentown. Things went well, so I bought another. They've been very good investments. I've gone on to buy real estate in Lynn Township and Jim Thorpe, as well.

I do almost none of the work of flipping a house and renting it out. I wanted to be an investor, not a landlord. Instead, I built a great team of contractors, property managers, lawyers, and accountants. I've developed good relationships with banks and private lenders also.

Staying focused on my goal—rather than trying to keep up with the younger investors in the industry—helped with my success. The houses I've bought have now been appraised for tens of thousands of dollars over what I paid for them. I've gotten my money back on the deals, plus more. The margins are very good.

Handling the Challenges

Issues come up. Construction can take longer and cost more than you anticipated. Tenants' lives blow up, which affects their ability to pay their rent. I'm a problem solver, so having obstacles to overcome suits me.

From the beginning, I tried to anticipate what costs would be. I was conservative with my estimates so I could cut costs or figure out how to absorb them when issues came up. I found that the most important thing to do when tenants were in crisis was to listen to them. Then I'd find out if we could come up with a plan for them to commit to what they can pay. Tenants are a source of income, and they're in a property that is my asset, so working with them to fix problems is good for my investment.

Having developed good relationships with my team and paying my bills on time over the years helps me work out a plan to solve problems like this. In a time of crisis, I can get a mortgage deferred through the bank for three months.

My goal of diversifying my income still stands. I am working on diversifying my real estate investments further by investing in duplexes or three- or four-unit buildings.

■ **My mentors:** I credit several people for putting me on a path to the success I've achieved today. One of my mentors was my grandfather, who managed a grocery store. After he retired at age 65, he spent the next 25 years working for the Chamber of Commerce. He was always involved, volunteering, and raising money for my community.

Another mentor I had early on was my high school gymnastics coach. He's the reason I never started smoking, and he expected everyone on the team to always do our best. If another team was better than us and beat us, it was okay as long as we performed at our best. He knew what I was capable of, and he pushed me a little more beyond what I thought I could do.

At Rodale, I worked in an environment that combined the vision of Bob Rodale with the practical and industry leading practices by Bob Teufel. Teufel's core team of executives helped me and countless other people launch their careers.

■ **How I structure my day:** I get up early, at 5 am. I spend the first couple of hours of each day listening to the news and podcasts while I eat breakfast. Then I get started on work. I've found I'm more productive during the day when I don't read or watch the news after 8 am. It wastes too much time, creates stress, and repeats itself too much all day. Watching the news after early morning is like eating junk food all day. It makes you feel lousy and doesn't feed your mind and spirit.

■ **What I read and listen to:** I regularly spend time reading articles and listening to podcasts by the real estate investment website BiggerPockets. I also read the *Wall Street Journal* and *BBC News* online every morning. I subscribe to PBS and listen to classical music as my background.

I listen to podcasts and read books by authors who feed my spirit as well as my mind. They include spiritual teacher Eckhart Tolle and author Malcolm Gladwell. One influential book I've read is *Rich Dad, Poor Dad* by Robert Kiyosaki.

■ **My hobbies and volunteer commitments:** I'm a master gardener volunteer with the Penn State Extension Service. A few projects have included teaching kids in middle and elementary schools in Allentown about how to start gardens as part of their science curriculum. I have also been a student of tai-chi for the past 11 years. My wife and I enjoy traveling and camping, and we traveled in our RV camper for 72 days in 2019. All of this makes for a diversified and interesting life.

I Bring Books to Life

Founding CEO, Bright Communications, in Hellertown

For as long as I could remember, my mom set the expectation that my sister and I would be the first in our family to go to college.

"I want you to learn how to use six syllable words in conversation," my mom joked.

Despite that expectation, there was never a discussion of how we would actually pay for our college education. When I heard of ROTC scholarships, it was the solution to a problem I was pretty sure I had.

I received 100 percent Army *and* Air Force ROTC scholarships. I chose the Army, and I attended the University of Pennsylvania, majoring in English. After college, I was selected to serve on active duty, and I was fortunate to be assigned to Fort Lewis, Washington, the number one most requested Army post at the time. I was an English major, so the Army assigned me to the chemical corps. But I was incredibly lucky that my military mentors gave me opportunities to use my writing and editing skills and passion. After my initial Army job as the nuclear, biological, chemical training officer for the 201st Military Intelligence Brigade, they moved me to be their assistant adjutant, then I was selected to be the Assistant Secretary for the General Staff (essentially their editor), then I worked as a writer on the staff newspaper.

In 1996, when my four-year Army commitment was up, I was pretty sure my wonderful Army assignments luck had run out. I moved home to the Lehigh Valley, where I had so many friends, family, and memories. My dream was to be a writer.

I got a job at Rodale. I started as a fact-checker. It wasn't my dream job, but I was young and eager to work my way up. Rodale had a large in-house writing staff at the time, and I was confident I could land a job there.

I loved working in the fact-checking department, which was run by three smart, nurturing women who complemented each other. The department was a group of around 30 females who were close friends as well as colleagues. A lot of our work was contacting doctors who were being quoted in the books for their approval. The doctors were smart, pleasant, and genuinely seemed happy to help us and our readers. A few years after I started at Rodale, the head editors offered an opportunity. Realizing that the 30 fact-checkers might have potential to grow into writers, they held a contest to compete for a writing position.

It was my chance. I threw my hat into the ring.

I submitted my writing piece and waited with excitement.

I was afraid things might not be going my way when I had my interview. Have you ever felt you just didn't click with someone? The chief editor was a well-traveled, worldly man with an elitist attitude. He asked me what kind of art I liked. I could count the number of art museums I'd visited by making a peace sign with my hand, and so my answer was, "Well, I pretty much like it all." That was the wrong answer.

A few days later, I crossed paths with the editor who was reviewing the writing assignments. I smiled at her in anticipation, hoping to hear good things about my submission.

"It wasn't what we were looking for," she said with a shake of her head.

I was crushed. I had always imagined I would be a writer! I had taken my shot, and I missed. I continued in the fact-checking job that I did still enjoy, then a few years later I was promoted to editor, and then project editor. I had skirted *around* the dream—like driving a beltway circle around a city when you can *see* the glittering lights, but not quite get there.

In 2004, I was working as a project editor: hiring, training, and managing freelancers. But inside I had baby fever. As I sat across the desk from my freelancers, mostly work-at-home moms, I thought, *Why can't I do that—work at home with my babies?*

My then-husband was quite concerned about the ebb and flow of freelance money. But I had an idea: I opened a new checking account for the business, and I'd deposit all income there. Then I'd pay myself a regular salary from it, just like when I was on staff, to even out the bumps in freelance pay. I got a freelance job to moonlight, finding the brass ring of freelance: an ongoing gig that I could work on as much or as little as I wanted. I was a writer for a publisher creating a series of books that featured tips by lots of people: Hundreds of Heads, the series was called. I was finally a writer.

After I had saved up a few weeks of my salary, I trusted my parachute and jumped. The transition was seamless because my boss at Rodale graciously agreed to let me freelance for them as did an editor who had moved from Rodale to another publisher. From day 1, I had plenty of freelance work.

I was extremely grateful that I could work at home. My son Tyler was born in 2005, and I got to spend every day with him. I wasn't minting money by any stretch of the imagination, but being at home with my son was priceless. Tyler was a colicky little guy. He cried a lot and didn't sleep much. I valued the advice of his pediatrician—who was also a mom of four, including twin babies. Looking back, I was functioning on so little sleep, I'm not sure how I could have worked outside the home at that time. His brother, Austin, was born in 2007. I was busier than ever, and even more glad to be home.

The Hundreds of Heads writing gig slowly wound down, so most of my work was copyediting, which I enjoyed. It comes naturally to me. My parents were both avid readers, and they developed a love of reading in me too. I can just "hear" when a words are grammatically correct—or not. I enjoy editing—I see it as organizing information. That's a skill that is easy for me, too, I love organizing things: spices in a drawer, clothes in closet, or words on a page.

But it's not writing. For me, writing feels like flying. It's magic. And still it eluded me. I couldn't turn town my steady stream of editing work to try to find writing work.

And so the yearning inside me kept being pushed down. Until one day, a phone call changed my life.

A literary agent I knew had called to tell me she just took a job at one of the big New York publishers to develop book series.

"So, Jennifer, if you ever have an idea for a book series, let me know," Karen said rather flippantly.

And the idea hit me like a bolt of lightning.

"Yes, actually I do have an idea," I replied. An idea that had been far in the back of my brain for a while now came rushing to the surface: I so valued my pediatrician's advice as a doctor-mom. What if we created a series of books featuring tips that doctor-moms used for their own families. I was pretty sure it had never been done before. Most health books featured the experience, the advice of just one doctor.

I pitched the idea to Karen, who took it to the company's Blue Sky meeting. They loved it, but they didn't love me.

"People want their medical advice from doctors," they said. "Not soccer moms."

Undaunted, I pitched the idea to my old colleagues at Rodale. They said the same thing.

I'm stubborn, but not stupid. So, I reached out to the most wonderful physician I had ever met: Rallie McAllister, MD, MPH, a family physician in Kentucky who had helped me with a project a few years back.

"I'd love to be a part of your books," she said.

We continued down the path of traditional publishing for a few months. We had interest from an agent in California who reminded me of Jerry McGuire.

"In a few months, I'll help you craft a proposal we can pitch to publishers," Steve said cheerfully.

A few months? I had already been striding down this path for six months by that point. I wanted to get started now! I was about to give up, when Dr. McAllister asked to talk by phone.

It was Mother's Day 2009.

"I think we should start our own company to publish these books," Dr. McAllister said.

I think you're nuts, I thought.

"I don't have the money to go without a salary," I explained. "Thank you for the idea, but I can't do it."

"I can find investors," she replied.

And so again I trusted my parachute and jumped—this time off what felt like a skyscraper. I interviewed 60 doctor-moms and wrote *The Mommy MD Guide to Pregnancy and Birth*. The book came together quickly—in just nine months, like a real baby. This was years before print on demand would turn publishing on its head, so we printed 3,000 books. They arrived on a very slow boat from Hong Kong, then a 50-foot tractor trailer that barely made it down my Hellertown, PA, alley to my garage.

When the driver tried to get the book pallet off the truck, he realized it was stuck. My then-husband went into the truck to help. Standing outside the truck, I could hear them inside yelling "Push! Push!"

A few minutes later, our books were birthed from the YRC Freight truck.

The Mommy MD Guide to Pregnancy and Birth was well received, and so a year later, we published *The Mommy MD Guide to Your Baby's First Year,* then *The Mommy MD Guide to the Toddler Years*. Then we did *The Mommy MD Guide to Losing Weight and Feeling Great*. These were big 512-page books! People's attention spans were becoming Twitterized, and I realized those big books were no longer marketable. So we focused our topics and created *The Mommy MD Guide to Getting Your Baby to Sleep, The Mommy MD Guide to Twins,* and *The Mommy MD Guide to Surviving Morning Sickness*. My dream had been realized: I was a writer.

By this time, our team of doctors had grown to more than 150! Our doctors started asking me if I could help them publish their books. Suddenly our self-publishing company became a "real" publishing company as we began publishing other people's books. We didn't have the mines of money of

I realized: I'm a book doula. I help bring books to life.

And I get to help writers bring their dreams to life.

traditional publishers in New York, so we began publishing by sharing costs and profits with our authors. This was a novel idea at the time.

Along the way, as our number of authors and books increased, our team grew, too. When I needed new talented team members, logically I reached out to my former Rodale friends. At various times, I've worked with more than 20 former Rodalians. I think of my company as "the new Rodale."

Once I opened the door to publishing other people's books, I began to realize that everyone has a story, and most of us yearn to write it, to share it. We grew from publishing one book a year from 2010 to 2016 to publishing 20 in 2020! Each of those books shares someone's story, and each of those books represents the tremendous opportunity I had to help the author bring it to life. I realized: I'm a book doula. I help bring books to life. And I get to help writers bring their dreams to life.

You Have a Business Goal; I Have an Idea!

Rita Guthrie, small business consultant and owner
of Open Door Public Relations

They don't call me the Idea Lady for nothing. I've built a career around helping clients reimagine their success using creative, out-of-the-box ideas that help propel their businesses to new levels.

I've worked with people to launch their concept from the beginning and expanded the thinking of high-achieving business owners to bring their remarkable success to new heights. I focus on brand consistency and clear messaging, engaging your target audience, and helping you increase your visibility by building your network.

For instance, consider one of my clients who ran a successful hair salon. She hosted networking events at her salon that were well attended by an awesome array of small business people. One day, she pulled me aside and asked, "Do you think I could do better?" I thought she could, and she hired me to consult on her upcoming affairs.

I helped her transform her events so that people were no longer standing in one place all evening. They were engaging with her staff and each other, learning about her salon and services, and she was growing her business—all while networking and helping a local charity.

We set it up this way: Her employees greeted people at the door, offered name tags, and invited guests to join the mailing list. Her menu of services was readily at hand. We staged the food to move people throughout the rooms. Appetizers, drinks, and desserts were spread out this time. As folks followed the food, they saw the entire salon and interacted more comfortably.

At one point during the evening, I got everyone's attention and with a warm welcome, I introduced the salon owner. She spoke for a few minutes and introduced her staff, who wore coordinated outfits to stand out from the guests. The event also raised awareness and money for a nonprofit organization. People brought a wish list item as their "admission ticket," and the representative from the organization also spoke briefly.

My client now grows her contact list and is getting more visibility with every event she hosts. Answering questions and booking a few appointments was a breeze now that they kept someone stationed at the desk during these events.

Keep in mind that getting folks to "cross the threshold" into your business space can be the first step in getting them to "know, like, and trust you," and possibly become a client or referral source.

Several years back, I received a call from Jill Strickland Brown, owner of the women's clothing boutique Frox. She brought me in to brainstorm details of theme nights that would bring in more prospective customers in a party-like atmosphere. She had a strong brand and knew exactly which type of clients shopped at her store. Her goal was to get more people to be curious about her shop.

We conjured up ideas for live music, cocktails, and snacks, within each theme and budget. Publicity stunts often worked. We wanted to get people in the door to walk around, engage, touch, taste, and have a memorable experience in a party-like atmosphere. Jill was also a marketing instigator in coordinating town-wide events on Friday nights. Collaboration was key.

On one occasion, I brought in a vineyard owner I knew whose quirkiness and knowledge made for a fun wine tasting night. For another event during the holidays, Jill brought in a violinist who sat in the shop's front window, with the lighting showcasing her beautiful instrument and the emotion on her face as she played. People on the street were pulled in from outside to hear the music, share a featured cocktail, and have a good time.

One of Jill's best weeks came from a back-to-school event—for parents. She served coffee and pastries during school hours. She got customers into the store with marketing that asked, "You bought your kids new backpacks and graphing calculators, but what did you buy for you?" Working moms clamored for her to hold the event on Saturday, too, so she did. The object wasn't to create a shopping event, but rather to boost exposure and a lure to return to get personal assistance in buying that ideal outfit or gift.

If business owners work for the success of those around us, our own success will follow.

Every client has different needs, and those needs will change over time. That's what makes my work so interesting. It is important to not only answer my clients' questions, but to help them know what other questions to ask.

How I Built a Talent for Ideas

Like many people, I didn't set out to do what I'm doing today. I earned a BA in studio art, specializing in textile design and fabrication. My first career was in supply management, systems analysis, and systems management for the Department of the Army at Fort Monmouth. Later I worked for a wholesale marketing company in the Lehigh Valley.

My hobby was to sing—and that changed everything. I sang in an acapella show chorus for 20 years and served on its board of directors for much of that time. When you're on a board of a nonprofit organization, everyone has to find something they're good at to keep the organization afloat. Over time, it became apparent that I was great at coming up with marketing ideas. My ideas brought people to our audience, raised funds, and recruited sponsors.

My fellow board members started calling me "the idea lady," and it stuck. Soon I heard, "Hey, Rita, I have a friend who's starting a business, but he doesn't know how to get the word out. Can you talk to him?" After the third person referred me for advice, I decided it was time to print business cards. That was in 2005.

Part of my success was instinct. I have great off-the-cuff ideas, and I'm a natural networker. The more people I know, the more connections I can make to help my clients.

What Sets My Work Apart

For me, it starts with being a good listener. Every client has different needs, and those needs will change over time. That's what makes my work so interesting. It is important to not only answer my clients' questions, but to help them know what other questions to ask.

I'm also a natural networker with an ever-expanding circle of influence, relationships, and contacts. I love connecting my clients with other people to form co-marketing partnerships that will help them reach their business goals.

- **One of my success secrets:** Part of my brand is that I make friends with everyone. When I see you at a mixer or business expo, I'll stop and chat and catch up. And then I'll drag you over to meet someone else I know who might be an asset to you. If business owners work for the success of those around us, our own success will follow.

- **What else I do:** Throughout the year, I do a lot of speaking engagements. My style is very interactive, so things stay pretty lively. Additionally, I host a monthly Coffee Talk. It is a relaxed discussion and networking event that is open to all. We cover such topics as generating new business opportunities, nailing your 30-second introduction, and ensuring that customer experience comes first. I also hold a semiannual Marketing Academy, which is a more intense, multiweek, small group program that I offer for business owners. And there are a few other programs and workshops targeting small business issues throughout the year.

   But the main part of my business is consulting on all different types of small business marketing and PR issues. I have worked with restaurants, doctors, health and fitness professionals, artists, sales people, engineers, and folks in real estate, construction, architecture, insurance, and technology. The variety and challenge make my work super fun and exciting.

- **Why collaboration is important in my industry:** I don't look at anyone as a competitor. When I meet others in my industry, it is my job to learn how our skills and offerings differ, or if we target a particular type of client. Why not become collaborators or referrals sources for one another?

- **What I read and listen to:** I'm a big fan of the NPR podcast *How I Built This*. The show explores how famous brands like Spanx, AirBNB, and Shake Shack came to be. Big brands didn't bust out of the gate with glorious notoriety. They had challenges just like the rest of us. They stumbled, they reimagined, and they failed before they emerged as famous success stories.

   An author I always refer to is Malcolm Gladwell, who wrote *The Tipping Point* and *Outliers*, among other books. It is fascinating to learn from him how and why certain things go viral. He urges us to rethink what we know. Did the Beatles or Bill Gates become enormously successful due to an incredibly lucky series of events, who they knew, or thousands of hours of practice? What's their story?

   And what's yours?

ABOUT THE
Local Luminaries

We are pleased to present the Local Luminaries' business and contact information here, in alphabetical order.

Pam Bartlett

Owner, Senior Helpers of the Lehigh Valley

www.seniorhelpers.com/pa/lehigh-valley

2814 Walbert Ave, Allentown, PA 18104

610-770-2036

pbartlett@seniorhelpers.com

Services offered: Non-medical in-home care for seniors

Jennifer Bright

Founding CEO, Bright Communications LLC

www.BrightCommunications.net

2336 Ridge Drive, Hellertown, PA 18055

610-216-0913

Jennifer@BrightCommunications.net

Social Media: Facebook: @BrightCommunicationsLLC

Services offered: We help experts and companies bring their books to life.

Jill Strickland Brown

Owner, Frox in Perkasie

www.froxperkasie.com/www.jillstricklandbrown.com

17 North 7th Street, Perkasie, PA 18944

behindthebuttonbook@gmail.com

Services offered: Online shopping, personal styling, and event speaking

Victor Cimerol

Owner, First United Land Transfer

www.FirstUnitedClosing.com

3500 Winchester Road, Suite 202, Allentown, PA 18104

610-433-0432

Victor@FirstUnitedClosing.com

Social media: Facebook: @FirstUnitedClosing

Instagram: @FirstUnitedClosing

Twitter: @FirstUnitedNow

Services offered: Settlement and title insurance services

Mary Evans

Owner, Evans Wealth Strategies

www.evansweathstrategies.com

134 Pennsylvania Avenue, Emmaus, PA 18049

610-421-8664

mary.evans@evanswealthstrategies.com

Social media: LinkedIn: @Mary Evans

Facebook: @Evans Wealth Strategies

Services offered: Financial planning, retirement services, and investment solutions

Samantha Ciotti Falcone, AIA, LEED AP

Owner/Architect, SCF ARCHITECTURE, LLC

www.scf-arch.com

22 South Second Street, Suite 301, Emmaus, PA 18049

610-297-0140

sam@scf-arch.com

Services offered: SCFA's goal is to provide down to earth, context-driven, environmentally-friendly architectural services for residential and commercial clients. We create architectural solutions for buildings and spaces that are beautiful, functional and environmentally responsible within our community. No project is too small (or large) to be well-designed.

Jeffrey French, CTS-D

Founder, French Curve, LLC

www.frenchcurve.net

Lehigh Valley, PA

610-442-0535

jeff@frenchcurve.net

Social media: French Curve, LLC | Facebook, Jeff French, CTS-D

Services offered: AV Workstations

Joshua Gillow

Owner, MasterPLAN Outdoor Living

www.mymasterplan.com

141 Karen Glen Way, Brodheadsville, PA 18322

610-628-2480

Joshua@mymasterplan.com

Social media: Facebook: @MasterPLANdesign

Services offered: Outdoor living design and construction

Pawl Good

Real Estate Investor, Good Community Properties

www.gcp-pa.com

PO Box 91, Whitehall, PA 18052

484-620-1228

pawl@gcp-pa.com

Social media: Facebook: @goodcommunityproperties

Services offered: We provide honest solutions for Pennsylvania investment property sellers who need to sell fast and investors looking to grow their real estate investment portfolios for better returns.

Steve Gingras

President, Valley Wide Signs & Graphics, JHM Signs, Sign Shop of the Poconos

www.valleywidesigns.com/www.jhmsigns.com/www.ssop.solutions

1745 West Allen Street, Allentown, PA 18104

1593 Springtown Road, Alpha, NJ 08865

610-841-4844

steveg@valleywidesigns.com

Social media: Facebook: @ValleyWideSigns&Graphics/@JHMSigns/@SignShopofthePoconos

Services Offered: Interior and Exterior signage for businesses, Production / Installation / Service

Rita Guthrie

Owner/idea lady, Open Door Public Relations

www.opendoorlv.com

610-703-5878

idealady@opendoorlv.com

Services offered: Consulting in marketing and public relations for small business, public speaking and workshops

Donna Hosfeld

Head Chick, Hosfeld Insurance LLC, InsuranceChix.com

www.hosfeldinsurance.com

www.insurancechix.com

339 Franklin Street, Alburtis, PA 18011

610-530-0304

Donna@HosfeldInsurance.com

Social media: Twitter: @hosfeldinsuranc
Facebook: @hosfeldinsurance, @insurancechix
LinkedIn: @donnahosfeld

Services offered: Auto, home, business, life insurance. We make insurance fun!

Carol Landis-Pierce

Realtor, Coldwell Banker Hearthside

610-417-0643

carol@cliffmlewis.com

Services offered: Real estate

Shelby Lawson

Owner, Lawson Accessories

www.Lawsonaccessories.com

484-275-0136

lawsonaccessories@gmail.com

13 E.Elizabeth Avenue, Bethlehem, PA 18018

Social media: Facebook: @lawsonaccessories
Instagram: @lawsonaccessories

Services offered:

- Custom sewing
- Ready to Wear
- At Home with Lawson Accessories
- Lawson Accessories Loungewear
- Yearly Fashion Flow Fashion Show at the Allentown Art Museum
- Looking forward to expanding to my hometowns of Greenville County SC
- Leaving a legacy of love, commitment, and faith for my daughter

Mike Lichtenberger

Group Executive and Chief Operating Officer, enTrust Merchant Services

www.entrustmerchant.com

Bethlehem, PA

610-849-.0818

mike@entrustmerchant.com

Services offered: Payment services and credit/debit card transaction processing. Commercial Business to Business payments. Point of Sale hardware/software for retail and restaurants

Dave Lin

Owner and principal agent, Linwood Forest Insurance Group LLC

www.linwoodforest.com

3312 7th Street, Unit 101, Whitehall, PA 18052

610-572-7322

dave@linwoodforest.com

Services offered: Property and casualty insurance

Erin Miller

Personal Development Mentor, Erin Joyce Co.

www.erinjoycementoring.com

Allentown, PA

215-852-17096

erin@erinjoyceco.com

Social media: Instagram: @erinjoyceco

Facebook: @erinjoyceco

Services offered: I provide mentorship through my one-on-one mentorship programs, do public speaking, webinars and host a podcast, *Same Boat Huddle*, to help deliver guidance and information to moms who suffer from anxiety and overwhelm. Through these avenues, these women can learn how to let go of the masculine structure of their time and to-dos by learning how to manage their energy with more flow and ease. I support mothers who are feeling stuck and lost, but have strong ambition and drive to create lives that they know they are worth living.

Carol-Anne Minski, PhD

President and founder, CMA Leadership Consultants

CMAleadershipconsultants.com

FocuswithDrC.com

209 Susquehanna Drive, Jim Thorpe PA 18229

215-688-2311

Cminski@cmaleadershipconsultants.com

Services offered: Leadership and career management coaching

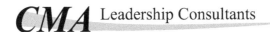

Jimmy Olang

Owner, The Brothers That Just Do Gutters

https://www.brothersgutters.com/pa

6323 Winside Drive, Bethlehem, PA 18017

610-285-7770

lehighvalleyoffice@brothersgutters.com

Social media: @brothersgutterslv

Services offered: Residential and commercial gutter installations, repairs and cleanings, and installation of gutter guard, soffit, and fascia.

Kathy Purcell, MT-BC

Director/President, Therapeutic Arts Group, Music Therapy Associates, Art Therapy Associates, ClearProtex

TherapeuticArtsGroup.com • MusicTherapyAssociates.com
ArtTherapyAssociates.org • ClearProtex.com

3437 MacArthur Road, Whitehall, PA 18052 • 1624 Schadt Avenue, Whitehall, PA 18052 • 610-740-9890

info@TherapeuticArtsGroup.com
Kathy@MusicTherapyAssociates.com

Social media: Facebook: @TherapeuticArtsGroup/
MusicTherapyAssociates /ArtTherapyAssociates /ClearProtex

Instagram: @clearprotex

Services offered: We provide individual and group music therapy, art therapy, music and art lessons and enrichment programs and ClearProtex—Clearly Protected Expressions personal protective equipment.

Specials for Success Reimagined Readers:
Mention the book and get 20% off any
services or ClearProtex CPE System

Rayne Reitnauer, CVT

Founder, Cold Nose Lodge LLC

www.coldnoselodge.com

235 W Penn Ave. Alburtis, PA 18011

610-965-3647

info@coldnoselodge.com

Social Media: Facebook: @cnlodge

Instagram: @coldnoselodge

Twitter: @coldnoselodge

Services offered: Dog daycare, training, boarding, bathing, supplies.

Ashley Russo

President/Founder, ASR Media

asrmediaproductions.com

410 Main Street, Hellertown, PA 18055

908-216-6100

info@asrmediaproductions.com

Social media: @ashleysrusso @thepeaktv

Services offered: Video, virtual event, and television production

Robert Sayre

Founder, SRS Real Estate Investments, LLC

www.linkedin.com/in/rob-sayre-3559772

New Tripoli, PA

Robert.sayre1@gmail.com

Social media: Facebook: @Robert.Sayre1

Twitter: Rsayre5615

Chris Schmidt

Chris Schmidt

VP of Operations, Keystone Running Store

www.keystonerunningstore.com

102 Mill Creek Road, Allentown, PA 18106

484-387-1258

hello@keystonerunningstore.com

Services offered: Specialize in fitting for your running and walking and everyday needs, fitting the Lehigh Valley two feet at a time

Specials for Success Reimagined readers: 10% off for anyone who has the book

Laurie Siebert, CPA, CFP®, AEP®

Valley National Financial Advisors

Sr. VP and Host of "Your Financial Choices" radio show

www.valleynationalgroup.com and www.yourfinancialchoices.com

1655 Valley Center Parkway, Ste. 100 , Bethlehem, PA 18017

610-868-9000

lsiebert@valleynationalgroup.com

Social media: LinkedIn: @Laurie Siebert

Services offered: Financial advisory services – providing insight, education and direction in discovering solutions for individuals for their financial, retirement, tax and estate planning needs.

Mike Sosnowski

PR Experience Guide, PRX Club

www.prxclub.com

P.O. Box 1043, Patillas, PR 00723

prexperienceclub@gmail.com

Social media: Instagram: @ prexperienceclub

Facebook: @PR Casa Marisol - PRX Club

Services offered: Luxury home rental and events: weddings, retreats, and team building

Ronee Welch

CEO/Founder, Sleeptastic Solutions

www.sleeptasticsolutions.com

Old Zionsville, PA

484-951-0902

ronee@sleeptasticsolutions.com

Social media: Facebook: Sleeptastic Solutions | Facebook; IG: Ronee Welch (@sleeptasticsolutions) · Instagram photos and videos; LinkedIn: Ronee Welch | LinkedIn

Services offered: I work with families on pediatric/adult sleep, lactation, nutrition, parenting, infant massage, postpartum doula support, and health/life/business issues.

Specials for Success Reimagined Readers: Save $50 on a full service package or $25% off any online course with the mention of this book!

Terree Yeagle

Photographer/Owner, The Moment Photography and Wear The Wonder

TheMomentPhoto.com & WearTheWonder.com

1444 Caspian Street

Allentown PA 18104

Terree@TheMomentPhoto.com Terree@WearTheWonder.com

Facebook: @wearthewonder

Instagram: @wearthewonder

Facebook: @TheMomentPhotography

Instagram: @themomentphoto

Services Offered: Lifestyle and business portraiture / Jewelry and decor

ABOUT THE
Photographer

Terree O'Neill Yeagle is a professional photographer and entrepreneur. Twenty-eight years ago, she began The Moment Photography, creating studio and location lifestyle and branding portraits. In 2015, she founded Wear The Wonder, a company she works with her oldest daughter, creating jewelry and décor accessories from her original nature photography.

Terree also enjoys dabbling in writing and has chronicled on Facebook the many life changes she has experienced in recent years. In so doing, she's discovered her enjoyment of inspiring others through the stories of simple life happenings. Next on her list, she hopes to combine her photography and love of writing into a book that would help others notice the wonder all around us and grow from an open-hearted approach to living.

Terree has two grandsons, and her three children are grown and live in varying places that she loves to visit and explore with them. She is embarking on a new life with a wonderful man to whom she recently became engaged. Life is for living, and Terree is excited for each moment ahead, but she always pauses in gratitude for the life she has already lived and the love that surrounds her and her family.

ABOUT THE
Curators

Jennifer Bright

 Jennifer is founding CEO of Bright Communications LLC and Momosa Publishing LLC, publisher of the popular Mommy MD Guides books and dozens of other books by expert authors and visionary brands.

Jennifer is a publisher, editor, and writer with more than 25 years of publishing experience. She has contributed to more than 150 books and published more than 100 magazine and newspaper articles.

She proudly served as a lieutenant in the U.S. Army for four years, stationed at Fort Lewis, Washington. Jennifer then worked for seven years on staff at Rodale before launching her own editorial business, Bright Communications LLC.

Jennifer's passion is helping parents raise healthier, happier families. She lives in Hellertown, Pennsylvania, with her fiancé. Together, they have five pairs of chickens, four sons, three cats, two dogs, and one amazing life. She can be reached at jennifer@brightcommunications.net.

Rita Guthrie

Rita is a small business consultant and has owned Open Door Public Relations since 2005. Specializing in marketing and public relations issues, she has helped more than a thousand business owners, and people in sales and nonprofits, increase their visibility and add layers of success to their marketing plans. Rita thrives on being a connector.

A native of Brooklyn, she also lived Upstate New York and at the Jersey Shore before coming to the Lehigh Valley in 1987. In her previous career, Rita worked in supply management, logistics, and systems analysis as a civilian employee of the Army at Fort Monmouth, New Jersey. After taking a few years to focus on parenting, Rita dabbled in wholesale marketing before launching her business.

Rita and her husband have three children and five grandchildren. She practices yoga and catches up on podcasts during her daily walks. Rita can be reached at idealady@opendoorlv.com.

Robert Sayre

Rob, a native of Boulder, Colorado moved to the East Coast in 1982 to work at a small book publishing company and to the Lehigh Valley in 1988 to work at Rodale, Inc. as the business manager of its book division, with many great leaders and coworkers. He is now semi-retired, an active investor in real estate, and a volunteer as a master gardener with the Penn State Extension Service, and he has studied and practiced tai chi for 11 years. He and his wife, Sally, a retired public-school teacher, have three children and five of the best grandchildren ever. They are as busy as ever, but they love controlling their own schedule and traveling in their Lance RV Camper.

CPSIA information can be obtained
at www.ICGtesting.com
Printed in the USA
BVHW050404100421
604637BV00019B/155